CONTEN

DEDICATION

To my mother Hannah.

To my wife to be.

To every woman who wants a good man.

BEFORE BOARDING

"Success is a journey, not a destination." - Arthur Ashe

I wrote this book for one reason. One. You and your girlfriends have dreamed about the concept, perhaps even argued about its existence, but "it," the concept, breathes, lives and remains in great health. The good man will literally arrive at your doorstep. Will you be in? Will you be ready?

I labored with this, toiled hard, because I wanted to make this book embody a sure-fire Home Run for success and not just a pick-me-up in difficult romantic and financial times. That said, you must understand that The Universe does not respond to your feelings, bank account or the economic situation; it responds to your adherence to its laws. With any desired result, the pursuer must follow guidelines, instructions, if you will, in order to attain The Prize. Understanding the need to show grace, decorum and elegance, I refrained from using a word in the book cover that my mentor often uses when issuing instructions. "Just follow the cottin' pickin' instructions Hanks." Tough words; enough to make even the most confident of us "feel" a little wounded. But remember what I said about feelings and The Universe? The truth remains, when I followed The Instructions, I got what I wanted. When I didn't, I met Trouble!

So, as the engineers make their final maintenance checks on Le Train de Bon Homme, I invoke similar words to those given to me by James Baldwin: It's. In. Your. Hands.

All Aboard…

Sincerely, Hanks

WARM UP

"Sow a thought, reap an act, sow an act, reap a character, sow a character, reap a destiny."- James Allen.

Poet WC Henley wrote: "I am the Master of my Fate, I am the Captain of my soul." These lines stand strong and have always stood strong because every one of us has the ability to control our thoughts and our thoughts determine our destiny. Our lives symbolise a series of effects which have their causes from our thoughts. Someone said in the course of a day, a person will have 60,000 thoughts. This simply means that you (your character) represent a culmination of thoughts. Character typically dictates why people reach certain levels. Character gets us to prestigious front doors, after that, character and qualifications will keep us in the room. "My husband and the next President of the United States, Barack Obama." If character gets us "there," thus determining our circumstances, this means that you can change your character and circumstances, simply by changing your thoughts. Therefore you and *you alone* can change your relationship status and also *you* in your relationship. When Senator Barack Obama won the presidential election, there existed mass hysteria and as one Canadian said, if we were quiet for some moments, we would hear the whole world applauding. From New York, Chicago, Washington DC, London, Kenya, one could feel the somewhat palpable euphoria and yet the United States still stood in two wars, the domestic economy had fallen into a recession, foreclosures and house repossessions abounded and yet on that Nov 5, 2008, people partied around the world, as Prince would say, like it were 1999. The artist Will.i.am even sang about "A New Day." What changed? Some may say nothing changed: bank accounts had the same amount of money in them, the unemployed remained unemployed and the broken front door handle was still broken. But on this night, something did happen. We felt change as we witnessed a shift in our collective consciousness. People in airports were kissing American passport holders. It seemed "cool" to be American again. What happened? Well, our thoughts happened.

They soared high, our confidence ran renewed, we knew we were on the brink of something very special and that effusive sentiment broke through loud and clear, as we held tight to a rightful belief that change had risen up and bit America from behind. "It's been a long time coming, but tonight because of what we did on this day, in this election, at this defining moment, change has come to America." And it has. It has. Latent in the euphoria, however, you have to acknowledge that "it": change; will require your active participation. "Barack and I talk about this all the time because when you're really trying to make serious change, you don't want people to get caught up in the emotion, because change isn't emotion, it's real work, organisation and strategy." Ladies, I'm asking you to hold that same belief, that your romantic relationship status *will* change, but strongly understand that it's not just emotion and the "feeling" you will derive from these pages that will bring "it": 'it's, real work.' Your work.

As a freshman student at Dartmouth College, one of my favorite Professors, William Binswanger, asked the class if they were to take a pill and that pill would turn them from white to black overnight, how much financial recompense would they ask for every *black* day they had to live. I know I definitely wrote it down, but I also believe I put my hand up and answered, "Nothing, because whatever I achieved as a white man, I could achieve as a black man, it may be harder, but I will get what I want." Feisty, confident, perhaps a tad arrogant, whatever the case, I derived this from my mother. I went on to insist that I have never been one to "race-hold," as Shelby Steele said in "Content of Our Character: A New Vision of Race in America," that is, hold my race against myself: to use my race to stop me from achieving. Ladies, just like President Obama never race-held, I implore you not to "situation-hold," by using the present day situation of a *seemingly* good man defecit and no man by your side issue, to stop you from achieving your dream of having a good man. The experts said President Obama had too few years behind him, "inexperienced," "untested," "too idealistic." But I bet you Michelle Obama never once wavered with the confidence she had in her good man. "You know in 16 years of mar-

6

riage, Barack hasn't once let me down." Michelle Obama cannot be the only woman who trusts in her man, but instead an indication of what happens when a woman does! If you, as women of excellence can believe *in* a good man, surely you have to know from the top of your hearts that you can *get* a good man. As change comes to America, romantic change has also arrived in your hands.

In Part One, I informed you that due to the direction I received from women of excellence when my life began to spiral downwards, I loved you and your mothers, since we all belong to the global network. Your words and encouragement represented your gift to me. The best present I can give to you isn't money, best wishes, or even myself, because I am a one woman man. The best I can give you all has to be the knowledge you need in order to attract a good man into your life. You may not have known that I relied on my alter-ego, Timothy, to get me through Part One, mainly because "The Great Lie" encompassed a tough message which I had to send to you, otherwise my involvement in your lives would remain futile. I never want women to feel anything other than pure joy when I address them, but to sacrifice truth on the altar of the present day "make me feel good" modus, may appeal to many, but would not serve the greater purpose. Part One represented the iron fist in the velvet glove, this Part Two represents just the iron fist. I sent Timothy on sabbatical, all the right chairs were placed at my table, the elevator went to the cranial top floor and I found myself in a rhythm, this time totally unhindered by a fear of hurting you. Timothy will return for perhaps the "How To Have A Nice Day" presentation, but for now I reserve this time for strictly business. "Instructions" stands tall. If you get offended by personal development and the prospect of hard work, then this second book-form presentation will surely leave you bitter, but if you have never shied away from sweat in order to achieve a goal, then you have caught the right train. As they say, this *is* the rub! So please join me in this, the second and final romantic relationships' journey. "Once more onto the breech, once more."

All Aboard Please, L'homme Expresse Departing!!!

STRETCHING:

"And reach 2, 3, 4, 5, 6, 7, 8 and stretch 2, 3, 4, 5, 6, 7, 8."

- Diana Ross

In "The Whole Woman," Dr Germaine Greer said she thought women were the dominant sex because men had to do all sorts of things to get their attention. In "The Great Lie," I used Oliver Wendell Holmes' insightful stipulation to inform you that every single thing which stood behind me, before me and within me, stood there because I heeded the strong counsel and direction of courageous, uncompromising women of excellence. I told you that at the age of 15, my grandmother, father and beloved mother had died in those painful 11 months, and I could only pray that I would meet women, like my mother, who would show me the way forward. Thankfully, I met them. I do not think men are weak, the man of character actually resembles a force for Obama Change, but aligning myself with the resilience and undeniable power of these women enabled me to live *My Life*. All those years ago, as I cried, devastated, bewildered *and* alone, I unknowingly began to absorb the words of *Gabrielle "dreams can come true, you know you've got to have them, you know you've got to be strong."* And just like that, e pluribus unum, out of many tragedies, came one focused mindset to follow the instructions given to me by these women and then go achieve the dreams. Ladies, as we get ready to embark on Part Two, if you also will just follow the instructions, you also will skip away with your dream. And not just a run of the mill, Pillsbury Dough Boy: you will have a man of character who may not run for The White House, but will change *your* life. If you don't follow them; well, you'll want a book purchase refund. This journey will not appeal to everyone, if you open someone else's mail, you will always be disappointed! And in fact, I implore the non serious to detrain now, for we will just waste each other's time otherwise. If you get off course, you'll probably remain miserable, tired and get old quickly. But if you stick to it, as I think you will, you'll pass go and collect $200 to boot! Stay with it ladies. "Why?" You may say. *Because You're Worth It*, I say. Part One set you up *for* love, Part Two represents The Closer, for those serious about winning. I wrote this for the woman with the choice behavioral life-approach modus in her left hand, and the responsibility baton club in her right. In other words, for the woman of excellence who has become somewhat militant about getting and keeping a good man.

Militant, yes militant.

We live in times where men have more accessibility to women than ever before. A man can chat up, date and break up with a woman without ever leaving the comfort of his room. Many women today have lowered their standards because of the *seeming* dearth of good men: "He'll do." "If I sleep with him maybe he'll stay." This has made it harder for those of you who want meaningful, long-lasting relationships and marriage. In the 80s and by a ratio of 3:1, men dominated video dating services, such that the service providers often gave women free memberships or reduced rates to offset the imbalance.[1] Additionally, the majority of men sought spouses not dates and hook ups. "In 1988, Great Expectations, the nation's largest dating service, surveyed its members and found that 93% of the men wanted within one year to have either a commitment with one person or marriage. Only 7% of the men said that they sought lots of different dates with different people."[2] Also in 1988, men who had sex with one partner were asked about their main concern after the hook up. Only 9% checked, "Was I good?" while 42% said they were wondering whether it could lead to a "committed relationship."[3] What a difference 20 years make? Today, the average man only wonders whether an appointment with a woman can lead to bed. A large percentage of men do not care about an "after" relationship. What happened? In four words, The Great Lie happened. Women took and continue to take their "Sex In The City" Samantha Jones' sexual liberation to the nth degree. Now, men beg to hook up and stay single. From the outside, it may appear that men do not need women in the same way they used to need them. But that's from outside. The playing field may have changed but the truth has not. There has never existed a time when men needed women more than they do today. The masses don't know it, but society does, as heinous crimes continue to soar. This need represents the great truth that men deny and sadly keep on denying. Therefore, the times we live in mean that you have to take measures that your grandmothers and great grandmothers did not have to consider. C'est la vie! Finally, there exists another place where you can use all that pent up competitive, feminist spirit. A happier you will mean a stronger society, a happier you, will mean stronger men.

Note, the woman who successfully follows the instructions will not have competed against other women on her journey, she will only have competed against herself. If you compete against others, then you will invariably just do enough to win, but if you compete against yourself, you will end up with personal bests and a greater caliber of man by your side. Remember you only need one. You might as well make him the best one possible! I have news for you. Despite the pity parties you and your girlfriends have about the lack of good men, they live and more importantly to you, they are looking. The tougher news that you must take on board relates to the undeniable fact that the better man, the larger his pool of qualified applicants. It is not enough for you to acknowledge your own beauty, intelligence, richness, believing that this puts you ahead of the next woman. The numbers do not add up. Men today have more choice then ever before. You have to be *your* personal best. I have lived a victory life because I took cues from you and competed against myself. In this endeavor, you must do what you first taught me.

This advice has great importance so that you don't end up with the same old story of pain and by the time you get through with the guy, you want to Lorena Bobbitt castrate him! Wayne felt the pain, but Lorena wore the blood. I'll save you the mess. Before we get started, let me tell you that this book bears little similarity to "The Rules." That great book typically told you things you should not do. I inform you about things you should do, in order to start developing a successful relationship or begin a marriage with a dream man, because *you* want to and not, as Alicia Silverstone once said, "just because he asked."

You've completed the hardest part by opening this book. Desire and passion for any project always represents the most necessary requirement for success. With desire and passion, you can literally do anything.

THE LAWS

The law is reason free from passion

- Aristotle

    This book has its foundation in laws. Laws govern The Universe, not hunches, hints, theories or entertaining writings, but instead, scientific fundaments and principles, set up from the beginning of time by a Supreme and Meticulous Being of Exact Order. I heard a great Law of Gravity example recently. The Law of Gravity says that when someone throws an object up, it must, by Law, come down. Taking this idea further, when you walk into a store and ask for a packet of your favorite gum, you exercise the Law of barter-exchange. The storeowner gives you the gum, in exchange, you give the storeowner your money. In the same way, by law, barter and exact order, when you make a decision to follow the instructions laid out in this book, you give the Universe permission to receive your payment and in exchange, give you what you want: a good man. Acquiring this book represents your first and most important payment. The Law of Control, Accident, Cause & Effect, Belief, Expectation, Correspondence, Karma/Life's Losers, Being and, as made famous by The Secret, the Law of Attraction, represent the main laws which govern the Universe. This Meticulous Being of Exact Order, who many of us call God, runs His Universe by these Laws and not by His love. Before you fidget, the 10 commandments do not encapsule these Laws. I am not inviting you to Sunday School here. Board games have rules devised so that each person has equal opportunity to win; in the same way, so does the Universe have rules which also allow anybody to win regardless of race, religion or creed. The Universe does not examine a person's religion or label to determine its next step. The storeowner will not ask for your religious or political affiliation before handing you the gum. Do the rules of Scrabble change, once the game discerns the religion of the player? For this journey, shake loose of the notion that if you just love, pray, cry to God, or become a "good person" in life, He will give you what you want. Tears do not impress Him. I've met some women who could cry on a dime when they started to recount their romantic histories, but they remain no closer to happiness than I do to Queen Victoria. Money does not impress Him. Some of the wealthiest women in the world flood online dating sites, fed up and skeptical about the men they meet as they go through their lives. But the Universe does not respond to desperation. The Universe responds only to adherence to its own rules and Laws. You have to adhere to The Laws and then you will surely get what you want. Laws, laws, let this one syllable mandate roll off your tongue. As you go on this journey, if that mandate becomes your cushion, and you can just hide yourself in them and them in you, even when frustration sets in, as it no doubt will, you will have that which you set out for. There remain no ifs, ands, or buts; as the sun rises in the morning, so will the woman who utilises The Laws get her good man. This is objective. When science enters, subjectivity exits. Laws; not love, not tears, not money, not fame, not opinions...laws! Many women allow a stock clerk mentality to pervade their thinking by erroneously believing that life has laid before them spinsterhood. That they just never had the right love cards dealt to them. They whine that romance represents one of those areas of their lives they have never and will never have any control over. That somehow God had it in for them or better yet, the Universe "called" them to singlehood. Sorry to shatter those time held beliefs, but nothing could be further from the truth. From Part One, do you remember the word for stale horse manure? It begins with C. Ladies, leave God out of it. Admittedly, as I traveled and studied, I got tired of women blaming God for their *own* predicaments. I witnessed some of the most brilliant and intelligent women at Dartmouth College, the Ivy of all Ivies, the bastion of intellectual curiosity, relinquishing their self-dignity rights by "shacking up" with whatever two legged monster came along and feigned interest. Hurried, harried and panicked because they didn't know the next time a man would desire them. Understand today, that God and The Universe has nothing to do with your situation; you do. The sooner you absorb this, the sooner you move on. Don't get me wrong, He orders everything (plays chess) and can switch up the most carefully laid plans in a nanosecond, but do not ever stand there in the bathroom wondering why God hasn't combed your hair, if you left your brush in the car.

All Aboard L'Expresse Bon Homme, calling at Syracuse, Roanoke VA, Fullerton, LA, Tokyo, Sydney, London, Saint Germain, Paris, Riverdale, Athens, Madrid, Nairobi and back to New York Citaaaaaay....last call, all aboard. First stop, Law Central.

A) The Law of Control

The Law of Control simply states that a person's self-esteem emanates from the exact degree that he or she feels in control of their life. The more you feel in control of your life, the more self-esteem you will have. The less in control of your life that you feel, the less self-esteem you will have.

B) The Law of Accident

The Law of Accident represents the inverse to The Law of Control. It states that everything occurring in an individual's life, happens by accident. This Law states that we feel badly about ourselves and have low self-esteem to the degree that we feel events and circumstances control our lives as opposed to the other way around. In other words, we are the victims of whatever else happens around us. If good things happen, then we benefit, but if bad things happen, we play the victim. A large portion of the population lives by this Law, until they realise, sometimes by Damascus Road experiences, that they actually have absolute control over their lives. Until an individual takes responsibility for the vast majority of what happens to them, they necessarily will live by The Law of Accident. The Instructions do not allow for the Law of Accident, everything that will occur in your life will happen by design, not luck or accident.

15

C) Law of Cause & Effect

Also known as the Iron Law of Human Destiny, the Law of Cause & Effect simply states that everything happens for a reason. It highlights the fact that all actions and inactions have consequences. Distilled down to the simplest possible terms, this law states that for every effect in one's life, there exists a specific cause. Sir Isaac Newton's third Law of Motion covers this law. It states that "for every action, there exists an equal and opposite reaction." The truly wonderful thing about this law is that by definition then, we should be able to manifest that which we truly want (the effect), simply by exerting the same causes that others before us have exerted and had success. If, for example, you were to hold your hand over a stove (the cause) the effect would be that your hand would burn and it would hurt! You will not put your hand over a stove again. Everything happens for a reason. In other words, your past, all the good and bad has brought you to this book. You can complain about your past, but what point would that serve? You are already here!

D) The Law of Belief

The Law of Belief states that whatever you believe with feeling and conviction becomes your reality. Not until you change your beliefs can you begin to change your reality and performance. Whether our beliefs have truth or not, we will automatically conduct our lives in a manner that will validate these beliefs. Your future will be determined by who and what you choose to believe.

E) Law of Expectation

The Law of Expectations tells us that whatever one expects, with confidence, becomes a self-fulfilling prophecy. We have the ability to somehow dictate the outcome of circumstances by our own self-talk and effectively "expect" our way to success. Since we talk to ourselves more than anybody else, one would expect high achievers to constantly talk to themselves positively, just as low achievers (losers) talk to themselves negatively. When one expects with confidence that good things will happen, they usually will. If, on the other hand, one expects a negative outcome to a situation, then the outcome will usually turn out negative. Our expectations play a key role in our own outcomes and they also have a remarkable effect on the people around us. What we expect from those around us determines our attitude toward them more than any other factor. In turn, the people around us tend to reflect our attitudes right back at us - whether the expectations and attitudes are positive or negative, good or bad.

F) The Law of Attraction

This Law states that we attract into our lives exactly what we predominantly think about. Positive thoughts yielding positive outcomes will attract positive people and situations. Negative thoughts yielding negative outcomes will attract the same. Harshly put, winners attract winners, losers connect smoothly with losers. The Law finds its basis in the fact that that The Universe and everything in it is simply vibrational energy in motion.

G) Law of Correspondence

The Law of Correspondence simply means that what happens on the outside tends to merely reflect what transpires on the inside. Your outer world will reflect your inner world. The adage "As within, so without" summates this Law. A sad individual, living in conflict with themselves, will always exhibit negative behaviors on the outside. A balanced individual (not necessarily happy) will exhibit positive behaviors. Sometimes, one can mask these negative behaviors and thoughts, but the true feelings will eventually reveal themselves. If you want to make your outside life better, the only way to accomplish this lies in changing what happens to you inside on a regular basis.

H) The Law of Karma/Life's Losers

The Law of Karma/Life's Losers simply states that what goes around comes around. There exist two energies in this world: positive and negative. If, in an interaction an individual hurls negativity at a person and into the atmosphere, the recipient can either join in and return the energy in a lower form or deflect it and send it back neutral or positive. Whatever the recipient sends out, it will return (boomerang back) to the sender and usually with a greater intensity, not necessarily at that time, but eventually. Life has winners and losers. There exist no middle lines. An individual either conducts their life with behaviors consistent with winners or behaviors consistent with losers. Winners deal with positivity and losers bathe in negativity. The goal of the loser lies in bringing as many other recruits into their negative world. We've heard the adage, "misery loves company." Losers live for company. They seek others who will host their negative energy either willingly or with a little provocation. Something happens in the ether when a loser enters it. They enter by free will, but *cannot* leave voluntarily, and just as we put the trash out on Thursday or Friday night, so too do winners have to put out losers. These interactions can become tiresome and leave the recipient bitter. Due to The Boomerang Effect where mass energy returns to its source regardless of its point of origin, the person who receives negativity remains wholly responsible for not continuing the cycle. By Law then, the cycle will schedule other losers into their life. Buddhism, Christianity, Hinduism, Scientology and so forth, do not have exclusivity to the process of non-negative response. The benefit of non-negative response simply fulfills a Law of the Universe.

I) The Law of Being

This Law states that we are our thoughts. Your thoughts have made your character and they, and they alone have brought you to this point without any luck or chance figured into the equation. This Law states that wrong, destructive, malicious thoughts can only breed negative circumstances and that right, constructive, altruistic, productive thoughts breed positive conditions. In this then, this Law emphasises the truth that we and we alone make ourselves. That with everything we have a choice upon what to dwell and for how long. We have the ability to choose whether a thought stays for just a while or whether we will allow it habitation in our minds.

"All achievements, whether in the business, intellectual, or spiritual world, are the result of definitely directed thought, are governed by the same law and are of the same method; the only difference lies in the object of attainment."- James Allen

INSTRUCTION ONE

State Your Want With

The Law of Attraction

"Give me a stock clerk with a goal and I'll show you a man who will make history; show me a man without a goal and I'll show you a stock clerk." - JC Penny

INSTRUCTION ONE
STATE YOUR WANT WITH THE LAW OF ATTRACTION

Act, speak, and think exactly what you want into your life. If you tell the Universe that you feel completely ecstatic as a single and you do not want a man, guess what? The Universe will oblige by law. To say you don't need a man right now represents one thing, but if you say that you do not *want* one, then you look for trouble! This stuff really works. I can tell you it works because in "The Great Lie," I stated to the readers and therefore The Universe, that I didn't want any friends. Since the day I wrote that 5 years ago, I haven't emerged close to making a friend, not one. The closest I've got to making friends is listening to Oprah *And* Friends on the radio and that really doesn't count. We live in a just and obliging Universe! Humor aside, even though this fact holds true, stating to The Universe what you want puts the process of attainment into action. This remains indisputable.

By picking up this book, you have dropped the GI Jane Act and declared to the world and yourself that you want a man. Women of Excellence or burgeoning women of excellence do this, they typically state what they want and then take measures to bring what they want into fruition. This project has a slight difference. With most business projects, you state the goals and then go after them. With this, you state the goal, make preparations for his arrival by your regime and then wait. Yes wait. If you don't wait you hinder the progress made. You wait because the Law of Attraction will bring him to you and the undoubtable change will represent the reward for waiting. You must have confidence in this Law, just like the others stated in this book… they all work!

The Law of Attraction Revisited

Remember Rhonda Byrne, author of The Secret? This wonderful Australian didn't write her best seller on The Law of Attraction just so she could fly Qantas first class! This woman wanted others to know what only a select few have known through The Ages. Do not embarrass *her* also by not stating to the Universe exactly what you want. The Law of Attraction, as you know, represents one of the Laws of the Universe, it also represents an important mental law. Simply put, we unconsciously attract what we think we deserve. We attract what we think about and what we put out. Every thought we have has a frequency and just like there will be a lot of static when tuning in a radio until you finally get to the desired station (in this case, the man caliber you want), our thoughts will also have static until we bring them in line with like vibrations. In "Think And Grow Rich," we learn that the woman who has successfully transferred her sex power to focus and drive (sexual transmutation) will walk differently, her tone of voice, handshake and whole demeanor will also have great difference to the woman who has not exercised transmutation. This greater appreciation and self-respect will also manifest itself in her thought vibrations of life, joy and contentment. Her thoughts will draw similar constructive, positive, healthy thoughts to her like a magnet. The Law of Attraction. "From the great storehouse of the ether, the human mind is constantly attracting vibrations that harmonize with that which dominates the mind. Any thought, idea, plan or purpose which one holds in one's mind, attracts from the vibrations of the ether a host of its relatives."[4] So each thought has a "dance" signal which men pick up. The woman who has her thoughts together will not have to do much at all: she will attract the man she wants from anywhere in the world, even by online dating. The pictures she takes, the words she writes should draw in its male equivalent. Her ability to transmute her sex energy will affect her pictures and words in cyberspace, just as it does her posture and handshake in the natural. Thought vibrations travel through space and speak to individuals in the form of words. For women and men who hardly have time to scratch their noses, let alone go out looking for dates, online dating represents one of the greatest inventions to humankind. The woman who doesn't capitalise on this form of dating misses out on an activity that saves time and presents concentrated information in seconds. Time is the operative word. You do not want to "run out of time," be "out of touch" and be "out of ideas" and then hope something sticks from "the spaghetti" you throw at the wall. You've got to have a method. Thoughts and words have a presence and an agenda. A man can reveal a great deal through his words. A man can act his way through a date, but it remains very difficult (eventually) to do the same through words. Remember this!

For ninety percent of the time the positive Law of Attraction occurs. But naturally, just like we have mentally stable people who represent gifts to this world, we also have unstable, sociopathic and as Donald Trump would say, "life's losers" who hover about. We all come across these criminals at one stage or another. No matter how learned an individual, it remains completely patronising for anybody, to try and tell another intelligent human being that all of what they attract into their lives is solely as a result of their thoughts. It's analogous to saying that all people are good people or all people are equal in talent. Light naturally attracts dark. Flies hover around radiated heat. Was not John Lennon a beacon of light? Did not Ronald Reagan shine as a communicative president? Yet they were both shot. Since time and memorial, celebrities have always had bodyguards. Why would a celebrity need a bodyguard, if the light they emitted only attracted good people? The stalker who finds you fascinating and the rapist who has no problem violating you, has emerged from a sick, debilitated mind. This vermin does not have a good heart. They have deep-seated sicknesses. For ninety percent of the time and as far as what depends on you, you will typically attract to you what you pervasively and subconsciously put out. As The Secret Intelligentsia all boldly stipulated in one way or another, your thinking does create your reality. So if you "think" right whilst following the other instructions, you will have a choice of men at your doorstep who will find you because of the Law of Attraction.

Oprah illustrates the power and truth of the Law of Attraction. Oprah has an estimated worth of $2.5 bn. Her money simply represents due recompense for her gift. Her gift attracted the money. This represents the Law of Attraction One, although, a gifted person does not have to state they want money, if they persist, money will eventually run them down as their gift provides for them. From a professional standpoint and aside from her broadcasting, Oprah did state early what she wanted. This want developed into a need which as she would admit became an obsession. By doing so, having honesty from the getgo about what she wanted, she prepared the ground for her desire to enter her life by the Law of Attraction. Note though, how she obsessed about her desire and then had the presence of mind and courage to let it go. The ability to obsess for what you want by building yourself up coupled with the courage to let go because you have done your part, will bring you exactly what you want. When you do this, you give the Meticulously Ordered Universe opportunity to take over:

> You're really responsible for your life, you are responsible for your life. I've known this since The Color Purple. In 1985, I did The Color Purple, prior to that I had read the book Larry (King). This is when I got The Secret thing but I didn't know it was called The Secret. I read the book The Color Purple, then went and got books for everybody else I knew. I was obsessed about this story, obsessed about it. I ate, slept, thought all the time about The Color Purple. I moved to Chicago. I get a call from a casting agent asking would I like to come and audition for a movie. I had never gotten a call in my life from anybody for a movie or anything like that. I said, is it The Color Purple? He says no, it's a movie called Moonsong. Well, I've been praying for The Color Purple...I go to the audition, of course it was The Color Purple. I audition. I don't hear anything for months and I go to this Fat Farm and I think it's because I'm fat. I was about 212lbs at the time and I think I didn't get the call back because I'm so fat, and I'm at this Fat Farm, and I'm praying and crying, saying to God, 'Help me let this go,' because I wanted to be in this movie so much, I wanted it I wanted it I wanted it, I thought I was going to be in the movie. There were all these signs that I should be in the movie and I go to this Fat Farm and I'm praying and crying and as I'm on the track singing the song, "I surrender all, I surrender all, all to

thee my Blessed Savior, I surrender all." I'm singin that song, praying and crying, a woman comes out to me and she says, on the track, it's raining, and she said there's a phone call for you and the phone call was Stephen Spielberg, saying I want to see you in my office, in California tomorrow. Now, what I learned from that, that moment absolutely changed my life forever because I had drawn (moving her hands in a circular motion) The Color Purple into my life. I didn't know Stephen Spielberg, I didn't know Quincy Jones, who saw me in Chicago in 1984. He was there for a lawsuit that was being filed against Michael Jackson because he was working on The Thriller Album and he saw me on AM Chicago and said that's Sophia. Now, I didn't know him. I didn't know anyone to do with that, but I knew I had drawn (circular motion with hands again) that into my life. It is very true that the way you think creates the reality for yourself...you really can change your own reality based on the way you think.

The Vision

If a young girl has a goal of medaling in the Olympics, she will have set up a series of steps to take in order to realise her dream. If a business woman wants to start her own fashion label, she will sit down, write a meticulous business plan with goal specifics, times, obstacles, attack methods and the potential benefits to her. This way her dream and vision moves closer to a reality. She cannot and will not leave her wealth accumulation to chance, good fortune or luck. Why then should you have any different resolve in order to achieve your dream of a good man? If you plan to have a business, you want the best possible business. You're not going to progress and then say, "That'll do." The mindset you cultivate in order to achieve your career and professional dreams equates to the exact mentality you will need to woo the good man into your life. Woo is the operative word here, because whilst you will have to have extreme proactivity with the way you live your life and what you do daily, you do not, I repeat, do not, have to go looking for him. What you do daily will determine what you become permanently because the secret of your future hides itself in your daily routine. So, if you do personal work and hit the panic button after a month, you have just returned to zero. Set in your mind that you've made a decision and you will not emerge out of this contract with yourself until you get what you want.

Acquiring a good man simply begins in the form of a thought. The mind which hosts the thought represents the only mind that can limit the caliber of man. Small, run of the mill man thoughts will breed the same. Intelligent, character-driven man thoughts will cause intelligent, character-driven men to move toward you. There remains little difference to starting a business. After you have written out what you want, you have to assess the obstacles (namely fatigue, frustration) that you will have to overcome. Unlike a business, where a lot depends on the co-operation of others, this project of acquiring a good man, pretty much depends entirely on you. Key here. Pause. Rewind. Re-read. *You* have the choice. *You* need to work. *You* bear the responsibility. If the man you want in your life will not find you attractive now, physically and most importantly, inwardly, in mind and thought, *you* have to do the work. In the '80s a program called *Fame* hit our screens. An immensely enjoyable show with many memorable moments, but one line in particular always seemed to stick. The intro ran and Debbie Allen would say to her students: "You've got big dreams, you want fame? Well fame costs and right here is where you start paying...with sweat." You guessed it, I am going there. If you want a good man in your life, he costs and by picking up this book, you've decided to start paying the price. Not with money necessarily, for the good man can provide for himself, has a vocation and does not need your money. He needs your love. This particular sort of payment involves time, preparation, concentrated effort, sweat.

I know some of you have had your hearts broken so many times and feel pessimistic at the thought of meeting a keeper, but I'm here to tell you that your past adversity has direct proportionality to your eventual and potential acquisition of and success with a good man. The vicissitudes of a woman's love relationships equates to the plight of any individual who makes a significant difference to society. Typically, this person has to go through devastating rejection only parelleled by other great movers and shakers. Don't waste your sufferings! We learn much more from our mistakes. We labor through tough times and heartaches. Let us ensure that we glean and log the hidden treasures found in our wilderness darknesses, as we also simultaneously strengthen our emotional musculature. Fulfill your life by having the tenacity to follow the instructions through to completion. We know throughout history that those people who persevere, without "jumping off the suicide cliff" or succumbing to failure's attractive call, usually end up with exactly what they purposed from the outset. From broadcasting juggeraught Oprah to media intelligence defined Madeleine Kernot to "I'm a mother first" First Lady Michelle Obama, "some are loud; most are quiet, but when the lights are switched off and the deck chairs folded up, these women (of excellence) end up with exactly what they want in life and exactly what they're supposed to have in life."[5] Ladies, if you can see the dream, you can have it. If you can see the good man, you can have him too, but you've got to see him first!

This Instruction fulfills Box:

INSTRUCTION #1

1) The Law of Attraction

2) The Law of Control: Stating what you want equates to taking control of your life.

3) The Law of Cause & Effect: Stating what you want (cause) represents the most important step to getting what you want (effect).

4) The Law of Belief: Stating what you want gives you confidence in the process and it changes the way you see your life. The successful attainment of your goal will become your reality.

5) The Law of Expectation: Stating what you want gives you confidence and you will then expect the process to bring you what you want.

6) The Law of Being: Stating what you want represents a positive, proactive thought and will breed a positive personal environment.

"I traveled the earth to see if I could glimpse a surviving whole woman. She would be a woman who did not exist to embody male sexual fantasies or rely upon a man to endow her with identity and social status, a woman who did not have to be beautiful who could be clever, who would grow in authority as she aged."- Germaine Greer

INSTRUCTION TWO

Develop Your Phf:

Become A Whole Woman

"The within is ceaselessly becoming the without. From the state of a woman's heart proceed the conditions of her life, thoughts blossom into deeds and deeds bear the fruitage of character and destiny."- James Allen

INSTRUCTION TWO

DEVELOP YOUR PHF: BECOME A WHOLE WOMAN

At the end of Part One, I said that the women who will "just put on their sneakers first and then start running" (the PHF) will have taken a major step to meeting their good men. The PHF stands for Personal Home Foundation and the thorough development of this foundation symbolises your move to wholeness and ultimately a good man. A woman needs wholeness first before she can attract a good man into her life. If she does not have wholeness, she will entertain a whole host of pretenders who will masquerade as good men. Wholeness takes time, effort, work, preparation. You have to do the work. This remains non-negotiable. A woman's adherence to The Great Lie, the idea that a woman gains power by hooking up, fractures any movement to wholeness because everytime a man leaves a woman he takes a little bit of her heart and good thoughts with him. If a good man enters a woman's life and he doesn't stay in the relationship when *she* wants him to, it simply means that she has not completed her wholeness work. Wholeness, the Personal Home Foundation, has five constituents.

Constituent #1: Your Heart

What kind of person are you? Are you a good person or are you desperately wicked? The messages that come from your heart to other people and to your mind have great importance because they will ultimately effect where you go. For obvious reasons, location remains vital if you intend to meet the man of your dreams. You will have to reach a place when your examined heart dictates where you go, as opposed to your needs leading you to the bar. Your heart will also determine how far you go in life and how fast you get there. Good men reside in all walks of life, but the condition of your heart will dictate the caliber of man you will have by your side. The extent to which a woman develops and conditions her heart lies in direct proportion to the man she will attract. Developed heart, developed man. Undeveloped heart, undeveloped man. The more her heart is developed, the greater the man. The less her heart is developed, the lesser the man. The late director Stanley Kubrick said, "The truth of a thing is the feel of it, not the think of it." Here Kubrick referred to movies, suggesting that the more an actor's heart worked and the less their intellect thought, the easier it remained for landmark performances to flow. Some women have worked extremely hard with their intellect and they naturally "think" deeply, but for the woman who lets her heart connect with a man and the less she "thinks," the quicker he will rush to stay by her side. This does not mean dumb down. It just means that after a certain point, the less you think and the more you use your heart, the better the outcome. When the good man finds you, "heart" your way and do not "think" your way along. Now, as a woman recently told me, "it's tough being a girl." Point taken, but once you realise the man in front of you has "keeper" written all over him and he wants you, jump with your heart. You'll get him, you'll keep him. Ultimately a man wants a female heart where he can rest his own troubles comfortably and know that the woman will not think him less of a man or stamp on his heart. Regardless of what you've heard, a man pines for love perhaps even more than you do and he measures this love by a woman's unwillingness to deceive him. Never forget that every man longs for a nest without thorns. A revisitation to life with his loving mother, but also obviously with a sexual component. The sooner you reveal to him that your heart represents a safe place for him, to rest and to rely upon, the sooner you will have him in your back pocket, with never an intention of jumping out! Unfortunately, those women who show the location of their hearts *literally*, as in, physically, remain no closer to the man, than the woman on the other side of the world he has never met. A woman can never win a man's heart with her body. Like the black widow spider that lures her prey into its web for its demise, so does the woman who tries to attract a man with her body schedule her own eventual pain and destruction. The true woman of excellence will never use her beauty as an instrument of persuasion. She understands that what attracts a man's attention does not always keep his respect and she unveils not the without but the within. Naturally yes, men are visually stimulated and because the majority of red-blooded men do not understand that the woman makes the man, oftentimes men place great importance on the physical even though deep down they also know the physical won't keep them around. Now you know what will.

The Great Truth That Men Deny And Sadly Keep On Denying

Many of you have had men cheat on you. Every effect has a cause and some women have driven men to look elsewhere because they didn't understand the sheer power of their words. These women have not understood that daily they either bring their men closer or create walls with their words. Many women, however, have fallen prey to men who firstly couldn't control themselves and secondly, continue to deny a great truth. Women are stronger than men. A woman can look at a man several times and even if she finds him extremely attractive, she can walk away. A man, typically will fall at the first sign of an interested leg! Without question a woman's body can whip a man and have him behave like a puppy dog. But with puppies, when you throw the tennis ball out for the dog, what does the obedient dog do? But if the dog sees another dog which interests him, what does he do then? He goes sniffing right? And a man will go sniffing, if a woman hasn't captured him with her heart. The body will lure him, but because of the man's weakness in this area, it can rarely keep him. This identifies one reason men cheat.

Fear represents the *main* reason men cheat. The majority of men will never admit it though. If a woman cheats on a man, the man will have supreme anger which represents a mask for the incisive, deep and life-threatening pain he feels. Women will hurt after an infidelity, but invariably come back stronger. This has to do with a woman's ability to express her pain completely and without restraint, letting her emotions of anger, denial, sorrow and breakthrough, perform the functions they exist to serve. In this way then, a woman's emotions, once assessed as a negative, become her greatest support system. When she feels angry, she will vent. When she harbors sadness, she will inform. Everything she will experience in this period of hurt, somebody on this planet earth will know! Men typically do not have this ability or support system. When a woman cheats on a man, the man will really hurt. If he makes it back at all, he usually will return as a monster ready to literally kick all women in the shins by vowing never to get burned again! There exists only one way a man can ensure that somebody doesn't cheat on him first! So even though the average man may never say it, he fears a woman cheating on him because he sees it as a challenge to his masculinity and he also doesn't quite know what he will do with his emotions if she cheats on him. Men have not learned how to handle their emotions productively and effectively. If a man feels pain who can he go to? His mates? Hardly. His mother? Perhaps. A doctor or psychiatrist? No. This represents a loss of face. Sports identifies one of the best endeavors a man can turn to without losing face. But sports, by its very nature sets up winners and losers. Not really appertising for a man who feels down in the dumps already. Not wanting to deal with the possibility of ever experiencing this intense pain with no refuge, he covers himself by having women on-the-go. "If Jane cheats on me, no big deal, I've got Alison. If Alison cheats on me, I've got Lisa." Men typically indulge in philandery because they do not want to get their hearts broken. So society has taught men to operate out of fear as opposed to confidence. Men and women alike have not informed men enough about The Great Truth. The vast majority of men and women do not know The Great Lie, and certainly the vast majority of men do not know The Great Truth. If men knew this truth more than just subconsciously, they would operate out of confidence. The average man doesn't know the repercussions for the man who hurts a woman defined as the Universe's greatest product. Women also hold the elusive combination key to the inner machinations of success, prosperity, influence, wealth and health. Most men do not know this either. Some of us do. "I would not be standing here tonight without the unyielding support of my best friend, the rock of our family, the love of my life, Michelle Obama."

Deliberately causing a woman to cry or hurt in anyway has the equivalent impact as poking The Meticulous Being of Exact Order in the eye. When that happens, He blinks and for a nanosecond, diverts His attention from the Order of the Universe to His eye and His greatest product. Over the last 20 years, the pokes have increased. Most men do not know that they cannot expect to enjoy any sort of comfort whilst continuing to bring pain to women. Their due recompense will literally chase them down. For some; it's a mid-life crisis, for others, it's the fall of a company, for other's yet; it's the humiliation of being forced out of a prestigious position, for others it's a life on the street and for many... it's jail!! I guarantee you somewhere along the line, an exposé of a man's fall from grace will reveal women who have shed tears due to his actions. Society has not told men that operating from confidence involves protecting and caring for the women in their lives. As I travel, it has astounded me how many men I have constantly asked: "Didn't you know?" Essentially, they don't know that exercising this type of confidence fosters the appropriate environment for *them* to achieve highly. Honoring women, as much as depends on me, has always represented my own law of the Universe. Society has not done a good job, but exercising wisdom, you as a woman of excellence have to inform any suitor you meet that you hold the key. I will always say my piece to men, but I cannot be everywhere. Ironically, when a man understands this and the more you reveal your heart to him, the more vulnerable he becomes to act out of his fear. The thought of you finding someone else now takes residence in his mind because never since his mother has he felt so emotionally safe. It feels weird, almost unmanly. He now worries because he knows you want a man. He doesn't realise that having the ability to tell the love of his life his concerns and requesting her feedback, represents strong and good man behavior, mainly because women are usually right! And what type of men does real society honor? Men who get it right. So it always benefits him to ask. A good man, a strong man, wants to be honored and he wants to get it right. "Barack Obama becomes the 44th president of the United States of America." But most men do not know what constitutes the truly strong man and neither do they care to admit dependency on a woman, so without having the conversation, *you* have to constantly reassure *him* that *you* are not going anywhere. Society today has taught men that a real man has women everywhere, where we know that a real man takes care of his one and only woman. When you reveal your heart, inform him about the positive prosperity key and the negative painful poke in The Boss's eye, where would a man possibly go? The answer is nowhere. His fear remains that *you* will go somewhere because he depends on you so much. You've got to "heart" your way to a man. Money, though necessary and useful, will not keep the right man. Some of the wealthiest women in the world have married several times and got the scars to prove it! Education will not keep him either. Many supremely educated women have been left distraught, returning to school for second and third degrees, in order to take their minds away from their pain of betrayal. Talent cannot either. The world exists full of supremely talented women; talented, sassy, beautiful and ALONE! As far as depends on you, your heart and ability to connect to his, represents your strongest attachment. An easily accessible heart remains the number one requisite for a woman who wants a good man. Note this.

The Heart's importance and ability

The messages you send your heart have even greater importance because they typically will dictate what you will do with your life. As long as you feed your heart with goodness, kindness and hope, you will stay vibrant and men will fall over trying to get to you. Women, in these 2000s have a difficult task, they have to toe the line between strong assertiveness in the reality of a tough business world, but at the same time have the tender heart which melts easily when wooed. No man wants to partner with Stonehenge!

I'm a vibe guy. I make my assessments very quickly. You're either on my list or not. Over these last 7 years, I have met more ugly-hearted women than I thought possible. But still, I've also met some women, through work and school, who needed not say a word. Goodness has a vibe, a good heart soars...it reigns. You need this vibe. It is non-negotiable, if you want a good man. In "The Great Lie," I re-counted how I had some women indirectly ask me if I'd like to go for a drink. "Alison…not even if Jesus was pouring it," came my non-ver-bal communication. I know you liked that one. I've met many women who have beauty written all over them but when they eventually re-veal their hearts, they resemble the backside of a rhino! Some women have such cold and bitter hearts that only a man looking to end his life would fill out an application.

Therefore this first constituent takes on even greater significance in your quest. Life has so many ups and downs, the condition of your heart (attitude) will determine how you handle them. What you read, watch and focus upon and for how long, will affect your heart and therefore future success. What goes in your heart, will affect what comes out of your mouth and what comes out of your mouth repre-sents ultimately your ability to first get a man and then keep him… get a man and then keep him. *Get a man and then keep him.* Admit-tedly many good hearts have found themselves alone. Many have said that they've tried and there was just nothing they could do about the situation. Nothing could be further from the truth, you can do something about it. You can turn your situation completely around with little help from anybody else, it starts and ends with you. When Napoleon Hill studied the ways of 500 millionaires, he also stated that both poverty and riches were just offsprings of thought. Rich-ness thoughts and poor thoughts emanated from the same well. That well calls itself the mind. Rich thoughts do not come from the head and poor thoughts from the stomach, both mentalities emanate form the same mind. Just as an individual has the capacity to "Think And Grow Rich," by thinking riches into their life, an individual has the ability to "Think And Grow Poor," (I hope this book is never writ-ten!). Just as you have the capacity to think about another player by your side, you also have the ability to think about a knight by your side. These thoughts offspring from the same mind. Where do you get your thoughts? Your thoughts come from your heart. Working on your heart therefore prepares you for a good man in the biggest way.

Constituent #2: Your Thoughts

Your thoughts represent the second constituent of the PHF and they determine your destiny. Emanating from your heart, it obviously means these first two PHF constituents remain intertwined. Have you ever thought about what you think about? You know the old adage, "You are what you eat?" Well, without question, you are also what you think? So if you think trash, you will be trash, if you think like a Queen, you will be a Queen. Your heart, your thoughts will determine where you go on a daily basis. Every single thing in life starts with a thought. Thoughts run the natural and supernatural world. Never to be discounted, they have incredible power. World War 2 started with a thought, progressed with a conversation and then ended after more thoughts. Thoughts represent New Beginnings and Cold Ends. They will put you in anything and bring you out of everything. This means that daily you make decisions, simple decisions, that will either move you closer to a good man or further away from him. Who would have thought that a simple decision to read a certain article or not read one, will move you to or away from a good man?

Your thoughts determine your actions. You will act based on what you think. If you have bad, destructive thoughts, you will act in the same way. Good thoughts bring to the fore good things. A culmination of thoughts represents character and typically you end up in life (places) where your character takes you. Thus your thoughts determine your circumstances. And where do your thoughts come from again? Your heart. If your heart determines your life, we can say so do your thoughts. Small thoughts, small life. Big thoughts, big life, no exceptions. "It's been an amazing year...so much more than I would ever have imagined. In February, Barack announced his candidacy in Springfield, Illinois, in front of the steps of the Old State Capital and it was freezing cold...it was about 20 below and the event was outside...I said no one's coming because it was too cold...that was the first time in a long time I had been wrong (laughs from audience), but 16,000 people showed up for his announcement...it was an amazing, inspirational day." Ladies, you have to understand that your thoughts are yours and no one else's and recognise the line of thinking you want to maintain, regardless of what other thoughts people try to give you. "But after that day, everybody said this race is over, they said there was no way that Barack Obama could win. There was a candidate that was inevitable...and we said, 'Wow really it's over, that's it.' We didn't have a chance to talk to anybody, nobody voted, we hadn't raised any money, but all the pundits said it was over." At this Carnegie Mellon University rally in 2008, Michelle Obama went on to describe how the pundits continued to set up barriers as to why her husband couldn't win. The pundits thought he couldn't raise the money. Six hundred and sixty million dollars later ($660m), the most money raised of any presidential campaign in history, obviously the Obamas thought differently. Next the pundits said that money wasn't important, that the true test of a strong candidacy was the ability to build a strong political organisation and "there was no way this guy Barack Obama, could build a political organisation to outmatch the political dynasty that had been building relationships around this country for decades." The pundits thought wrong again because Barack Obama using his Community Organiser skills "built the largest network anyone has ever seen in politics." Ooops! Once again the Obamas thought differently. Then the pundits came back, "Oh organisation's not important, everybody can build an organisation, the true test of a candidate was whether they could win Iowa, Iowa was the test...Barack won Iowa overwhelmingly." Then the pundits said, "Iowa's not important...because it's just a caucus, they don't count, this was now a national race." Lah dee dah dee daaah...and you know the rest is *their* story. I gave you this example in depth because how many times have your girlfriends said that it's pointless waiting for a man, they're all crooked? How many times have you been told to give up? How many times have you been told that you might as well just get a sperm donor because you won't find a good man with whom to have a baby? As you read this book, never despise the day of small beginnings. All successes start with a thought. It all counts, your actions determine what comes into or moves out of your life and with what frequency. The quality of your life has complete connection to your thoughts. They determine everything in your day, from what you do, to whom you speak to, as remains dependent on you. If you cannot find a way to host constructive, uplifting thoughts with an uncommon regularity, you will automatically by default, think unhealthy, destructive thoughts which can help no one else, least of all you. You have to find a way to monitor your thoughts. In Barack Obama's case, they determined where he went and how fast he got there. In your situation, your thoughts will determine the man you get and how fast you get him!

Constituent #3: Your Character

Who are you? What do you stand for? Anybody can look good front stage and in front of a camera, but who are you back stage, in the room alone by yourself with no one around. Our hearts represent our character and who we 'truly' are inside. Our character represents a constancy of our basic thoughts. When people say that someone did something which they consider "out of character," they communicate that they would never have *thought* that the individual in question would have done a certain thing; because they assumed that the individual didn't harbor such *thoughts*. Our day-to-day thoughts, whether good or bad, work together to give us a character. Why is your character important in meeting a good man? Well, it may not be important in meeting him, I mean your body can help you meet him, but it is your character, who you are, which will enable you to keep him. As dictated by the original equation at the outset of this chapter, our character pushes us to a particular destiny. In this way then, it is therefore the condition of our hearts (our character and basic thoughts) which determines the quality of our lives. We have three selves. The public self which represents what we show to the world, the private self which signifies what we reveal at home, back stage away from people and the deep inner self which identifies who we really are. The deep inner self, the constancy of our thoughts combined with the private self equals our character. Your character represents a collection of your thoughts, so you change your character, by changing your thoughts. I am slow on many things and you know I am crazy because I actually like revealing that I am slow, but I am not slow on a person's character. I derived this from my mother. As I can remember, we never actually had a conversation about this, I just watched her. She taught me that a person doesn't even need to speak to show their intentions. My mother hardly spoke, very quiet and yet she knew someone by their vibe. She knew them and so when they spoke, I knew the person just confirmed to my mother what she already knew about them. I've met some alligators in my life, male and female, there exists more hope for the last piece of chicken in my fridge than for these people to ever change their characters and have a place in my life. Why? Because they have difficulty changing their thoughts.

Constituent #4: Your Integrity

Integrity is when your actions fit your words. Be the kind of person who says what they will do and then does exactly what they said they would do. There's no place for phoniness or duplicity in your quest to meet a good man. Men may act like they're only interested in one thing and I assure you, if a man approaches you and you are not genuine, you go from the woman with whom he may have thought of settling down to the woman with whom he simply just wants to sleep. Why? A man wants a real woman by his side, he doesn't want a phony or a showcase theater. If he cannot see a real you, then how can he ever feel comfortable in laying his most intimate thoughts with you? The Greek Philosopher Heraclitus said, "Your integrity is your destiny, it is the light that guides your way." Once again we can see that your integrity, just like your heart will determine where you go, as in location and also where you go, as in status, and how fast you get there. Doesn't mean that you have to relay all your life, but when you say something mean it and mean what you say.

Constituent #5: Your Honesty

Honesty, when your words fit your actions, represents the fifth essential for your Personal Home Foundation. James F. Bell, General Mills founder said: "Honesty is not only the best policy, but the only possible policy from the standpoint of business relations...If we expect and demand virtue and honor in others, the flame of both must burn brightly within ourselves and shed their light to illuminate the erstwhile dark corners of distrust and dishonesty." Out of ten people walking along the street eight will lie habitually, it benefits you greatly to be one of those two. I do not think there exists a woman on earth who does not want honesty from the man in her life. Men may not say it, but they want the same thing. Deception and lies have a similar effect to him and actually even worse. This occurs because women have an ability to lie and nobody would be the wiser. Men are pretty good, but women wrote the book! Acting comes extremely naturally to women, so naturally the average onlooker couldn't tell. In order for a woman to get that honesty from a man, she has to be what she wants to see.

Your heart, thoughts, character, integrity and your honesty, these constitute your PHF and your foundation must be in place in order for you to become dangerous in the "Attract a good man market." It's important to understand that in order to have financial wealth, you will need many thousands of dollar bills, but to be rich romantically and "full up" in your deepest heart's song, you only need just one good man. One. Money typically finds the woman who works with her gift and in her element. She has to work hard though, because millions of dollars do not fall from the sky. In the same way, when you have achieved wholeness, good men will find you. You also have to work hard because especially today, good men do not fall from the sky. Once in a while, the loser will appear on the scene namely because of the light you show, but as you develop wholeness and become comfortable in your new self, you will see the good men flocking to you.

This Instruction fulfills Box:

INSTRUCTION #2

A) The Law of Control: You cannot have a great life unless you have a grounded life. Grounded in the sense that you know what comprises you, what "you" means, your essence and core. Gravitas, bearing, a center devoid of everything negative, this represents a great life. Mother Theresa? Well, I am saying that you have to constantly work on your shortcomings so as to reach a point such that if people can't get along with you, there exists something wrong with *them*. You bring nothing but positivity to the table, you are who you are and you make no excuse for your inner self. The list remains exhaustive, but in order to have a great life, you have to find a way to deal with these things. If you harbor any of them they will taint you...you have to be happy with who you are and to be this way, you have to constantly monitor your daily motivations. Why do you do certain things, what are your motives? If you can examine yourself daily without exception, you will move closer to wholeness and a great life. That said, if you know that your motives are right, you gain a confidence and healthy self-esteem. Self-esteem is simply confidence in you. By this then, you have the ability to raise your esteem levels, higher self-esteem means greater living because you then operate by a compass, you literally control your life.

B) The Law of Correspondence: If you have reached wholeness, you will exude wholeness. Whole people are attractive, they have balance and they reflect that balance daily.

C) The Iron Law of Human Destiny, the Law of Cause & Effect simply states that everything happens for a reason. Your wholeness, self-awareness will cause wholistic experiences to enter into your life, thus mapping your destiny. The degree to which you strive for wholeness equates to the degree to which you realise your potential and have meaning. Many do great things in life and make significant contributions to the world, but they still do not enjoy their lives as they should because they remain far from whole.

D) The Law of Belief: If you rightly believe that a quest for wholeness will move you forward in significant ways, that will occur.

E) Law of Expectation: if you rightly expect a quest for wholeness will move you forward in significant ways, that will occur. By this then, you will know if you have moved off center.

F) The Law of Attraction: A movement to wholeness will not only attract whole men, but it will also attract men with serious flaws. They need you to fill their holes.

G) The Law of Karma...If you throw wholeness out, wholeness comes back.

H) The Law of Being: You are wholeness.

INSTRUCTION THREE

Hold the Power:

Know the Great Lie

INSTRUCTION THREE
HOLD THE POWER: KNOW THE GREAT LIE

Power. It's all about power. Oprah Winfrey told her studio audience that in her twenties she unknowingly gave her power away to men. "You are nothing when you give your power over to men." In "The Whole Woman," feminist icon Germaine Greer insisted: "The female body is not our enemy, but our strength…" Social psychologist Monica Longmore noted: "Who will teach them that there is power in holding back?" In "Sex, Art and American Culture," Italian feminist Camille Paglia expressed: "I do feel that women have to realize their sexual power over men. This is part of our power."

Ladies, your successful acquisition of a good man will require two things. You will need to hold great power over him, simply defined as the ability to influence another, and you will also require the man to deeply respect you. If either of these two components do not reside in your birthday suit wardrobe (the real you, without money, clothes or status) you will continually remain on course for more romantic drama and pain. In these days we live in, the woman who "bags" a good man has great power and will garner deep respect, not just from her man, but also from masses of women. There seemingly exists a dearth of good men that her attainment of one will automatically elevate her to genius status! With this in mind, there exists concentrated information in Napoleon Hill's words. He effectively said that the woman who controls/harnesses her "sex emotion," by Oprah's contention also, has power. This power therefore elevates her to genius status. After studying over 500 wealthy men, Hill stated that scientific research revealed that high achieving men typically had "highly developed sex natures." Though men and women have distinct, fundamental, psychological, physiological, chemical and chromosomal differences, they stand exactly alike with regards to the results of channeled sex emotion. High achievers have learned to turn the most powerful of emotions into the accumulation of wealth and contributive societal impact. Howard Gardner, author of

"Multiple Intelligences," insisted that there are 7 ways of measuring intelligence and thus for our purposes here, let us state that there exist 7 ways of measuring genius. Mathematical intelligence (Einstein), Musical (Beethoven), Interpersonal (Oprah), Intrapersonal (Victor Frankl), Linguistic (Maya Angelou), Kinesthetic (Michael Jordan), Visual (Leonardo Da Vinci). Each of these individuals represented and represent genii in their particular calling. Upon discovering the dedication and desire required for the successful completions of their vocations, without exception, they all drove their sex power into their work.

How does a woman hold even more power? How does she gain even more respect?

Power first: The power-seeking woman will avoid the hook up. If you have hooked up before; once, twice, dozens of times, it really has nothing to do with me, it's none of my business, but if that is the case and you are serious about having a good man, today does represent "A New Day." I'd sooner see you as a Die Hard Serial Monogamist than hook up with one of those rug-rats. In "The Great Lie," I enumerated the traits of the woman of excellence compared to the Needy woman. I also outlined the power distributions for those women who hook up and those who do not. I will summarise it here. As I pointed out, if we combine the intellectual, emotional and sexual power of a woman with her women's intuition and her ability to give life, she receives a rating of 3 times a man. In her classic, "The Female Eunuch," Germaine Greer said, "we are certainly our bodies." The French Politician, Anthelme-Brillat Savarin noted, "Tell me what you eat and I will tell you what you are." From this we get that popular adage, "you are what you eat." James Allen, author of "As A Man Thinketh" said, "a (hu)man is literally what he thinks." Combining 1, 2 and 3; we can conclude that a woman is what she thinks, what she eats and she is certainly what she does with her body. Therefore, when a woman enters the hook up, she literally loses all of her power by going from **3 Times A Man to 5 DOWN** to him, in terms of power.

Let us go further with the power definition: one as the ability to influence another; the other, as a feeling of personal empowerment (gravitas). Women want an emotional connection combined with the physical connection when they have intercourse. In this regard, because the hook up represents a one-time endeavor, the woman who hooks up, may get what she wants physically, but she does not get what she wants emotionally. She therefore loses. Some women say that they can handle a one night stand, but asking a woman to have a level of comfort with this type of arrangement is analogous to putting a fish in water and commanding it not to swim. Any individual who doesn't get what they want in a relationship feels weakened in their ability to influence their partner and thus also loses ground, gravitas in the relationship and within themselves. The woman who hooks up does not get what she wants. **1 DOWN**. The woman who enters the hook up also swings in emotion. It remains almost impossible for a woman to have a sexual encounter without taking her emotions with her. She will therefore swing in emotions, something detrimental to her ability to influence a man, since she will now talk from a position of weakness and not enjoy strong personal power or standing in the relationship. **2 DOWN**. The woman in the hook up becomes discardable. When a woman goes from one relationship (boyfriend-girlfriend) to another, the new guy who gains her feels happy: "Can't believe you're single, I would have given my right arm to stay with you." But when a woman goes from bed to bed, the man can't wait to discard her after he gets what he wants. At Dartmouth, when a male student wanted to hook up, he would say that he wanted to spit game. The hook up represented the game, the woman represented the spit. What do we do with spit? Typically, we wash it down the sink or hurl it to the side of the road as some discardable, unwanted mucous. **3 DOWN**. Dr David Buss from The University of Texas conducted a study with men and women. He found that when a man had sex with a woman he felt less attracted to her afterwards, but when a woman had sex with a man she felt more attracted to him afterwards. The woman obviously loses her ability to influence because the man no longer has the same attraction to her and she does not have equal footing in the relationship, harboring feelings of disempowerment and confusion. **4 DOWN**. Dr David Buss also said that a man's primary objective is to impregnate somebody who is female. In other words, most men just want to sow their royal oats. In order to do this, he needs an empty bed. If the woman doesn't leave voluntarily (Samantha), he will send her away. She loses power when he does this. **5 DOWN**.

5 DOWN SUMMATION BOX

When a woman hooks up:

1) She doesn't get what she wants

2) She swings in emotion

3) She's devalued to a "Spit"

4) She is more attracted to the man while he is less attracted to her

5) She is sent away

When we contrast this with the power attribution for the woman who doesn't hook up, the power loss becomes more apparent. In "Crunch Time," Ken Lindner also mentioned the positive affects on goal attainment when an individual channeled their emotional and sexual energies. If a woman wants to reach her full potential whether academically, artistically or professionally, it only makes sense that she doesn't hook up and "divert" that energy to situations which can only bring damage. The sex emotion represents the most potent of all the emotions. It takes some of the fight out of a man, this remains the reason why boxers typically refrain from sex months before a big fight. In sexual intercourse, a woman dispenses more energy resources than the man and so when a woman abuses her sex power, her actions remove some of her own drive and passion and due to this she rarely achieves what she can in life. A woman is what she thinks, eats and what she does with her sex life. Matter of factly, men and women both are what they eat, think and do with their sex lives. Sadly, the majority of men have not understood this. Nietzsche said: "the degree and essential nature of any human being's sexuality extends into the highest pinnacle of her spirit." The individual who goes from A to B to C to D to E to F, without a breath is like a weed in the wind, the perpetual "feel-good feeler" who has few boundaries and whose life will mirror the same. Many women understand this. There exists no rock, no compass to which to return, anything goes. Samantha didn't tell Kristin, Charlotte and Miranda that a wandering sex life produces a wandering life period. Harvard technocrat Esther Dyson, pioneer and former owner of EDventure holdings who sold her company to take up newer challenges in private aviation, space and health care, noted the personal, deleterious effects when a person abuses their power: "People behave badly because they lack power over their lives. I know it sounds simplistic, but people without control over their lives have stress." Here Dyson necessarily may not refer to sex power per se, but as we acknowledge that we respond to life circumstances based on emotion, as our primary force and that the sex emotion has the greatest power, it follows sex emotion will serve as a rudder to our lives. Once a person takes charge of their sex drive, they take charge of their life. **1 UP.** Note that there exists no difference in the level of achievement between the man and the woman who channels their sex drives. The acquisition of a good man *will* require the same type of control from a woman. The woman who harnesses this sex energy, moves closer to the good man. She somehow understands whether by study or intuitively that her ability to control her sex drive remains directly proportional to the man she will have at her side. This will occur if she does not hit the panic button when the man doesn't appear on the scene within her own constructed timetable. Through the course of her transmutation, and provided she follows the other instructions, she will literally have men fighting over her. This woman will also never have to pursue a man, with her sex drive in check, she will never have to do so! Despite what "Sex In The City" Samantha demonstrated and what any New Ager will agree with, the average man would like to call the woman. When this woman steps into a room, she will draw men to her without even smiling or opening her mouth. Men who ordinarily wouldn't go for redheads will literally fly over to meet a sexual transmutation-woman. "When a happy, secure, complete woman finally sits down at the table with her credits in hand; her mind, BODY and soul in tact, then I ask you...'Who Has The Power?'"[6] Do you ever see average looking women with so called heartthrobs? The same applies to men, the average looking man who taps into this will also have model-type women falling all over him, even if he looks like Chronomacken! He could be bald, broke and battered, but if the boy's got his sex emotion in check, he will have women falling all over him. It is exactly the same for women. Regardless of what you hear, no man wants a woman who has slept around. Men have a virgin complex, in that every man likes to delusionally believe that the woman he sleeps with, has never slept with another man and does not have the capacity to sleep with another man. If a man doesn't respect a woman, he will regard the woman as nothing more man than a good time, "booty call." He may call her girlfriend, but he really means *guaranteed booty call*. To the average man, life just doesn't get any better than a series of uncomplicated booty "calls." Everytime she sleeps with a man, outside of the true love paradigm, that represents one less level of good man she will have. Good men want powerful women, both in the sex and self-knowledge category. Socrates said "Know thyself." The woman who exercises sexual transmutation will know what she wants in her life. Women who busy themselves with their lives, know what they want, know who they are and therefore typically will not settle. They have a picture of the exact career and man they want. Singleness allows for this growth, sexual control fosters this development, they have inner peace and a woman with inner peace can say no to a loser as easily as she can say yes to a winner. Tragically, the woman who believes The Great Lie will always have difficulty defining who she is and what she represents away from a man. And when a woman doesn't know who she is, she will join up with anybody." Ripe for the picking, by the fountains, at the bus shelter, back of the car, on the couch at a party, *Any Idiot Can Apply.*" [7] This line explains why some women will never realise their good man dream, but it also demonstrates why some will. If a woman knows who she is and why she is, so will he. If she doesn't, neither will the man and what remains worse, he will never want to know. Living with a man who does not care about his woman's personal development equates to the feminine end of suicide fullstop. Women want the candlelight dinners. It makes no sense then for an over-the-top feminist to irritatingly put forward that today's women want femaleists' labels: women who behave more promiscuously and aggressively than men with regards to sex. One Great Lie generally leads to another. The woman who wears the femaleist title, will never wear the tiara! It remains a big fallacy that a woman can sleep her way to a good man. She'll sleep her way to disappointment and maybe AIDS, but definitely not to a good man. The woman who avoids the hook up once she knows better, gets the best man, she gets the good man. **2 UP.** Masters and Johnson-trained therapist Dagmar O'Connor and author of "How to Make Love to The Same Person for the Rest of Your Life" noted that "sex has the potential to be more thrilling, more varied, more satisfying in every way than any other sexual arrangement you can think of." Sex within a monogamous relationship is more fulfilling than sex in a one night stand. **3 UP.** Everytime a woman has sex, she gives more of herself physically and emotionally. In "101 Ways To Get And Keep His Attention," Michelle McKinney Hammond stated the inevitability when a woman hooks up: "when she has sex, she's giving her body and spirit. And when that man walks away, he takes a piece of her spirit that she can never get back." Not hooking up allows a woman not to fragment herself. She can remain whole. This is power. **4 UP.** The woman who doesn't hook up will never have to dread that important conversation with her daughter. With confidence, she can tell her daughter about her own life and she will not even have to talk anymore, because her daughter will see that she has a good man by her side and has had a fulfilled life. The woman who does not dread the mother-daughter conversation has power. **5 UP.** "It is very little to me," said suffragist Lucy Stone in 1855, "to have the right to vote, to own property, etcetera, if I may not keep my body, and its uses, in my absolute right." Voting represents power, owning property represents a form of power, hooking up does not represent power. When a woman crosses her legs, as my Aunty McCullough would say, she will have men running all over town for her. The woman who doesn't hook up, retains the power she had, but also gains power. **6 UP.**

Conclusion:

6 UP SUMMATION BOX

<u>**When a woman doesn't hook up:**</u>

1) She attains her goals in a big way

2) She gets The Best Man:

3) She has the most fulfilling sex.

4) She becomes A Whole Person

5) She will not dread "The Conversation" as a mother

6) She retains and gains power.

The participation of a woman in the hook up, with all its various downsides renders a woman completely powerless. Already 3 Times A Man, a woman who hooks up moves 5 DOWN in terms of her overall power, as opposed to the woman who doesn't hook up who rises to 6 UP, having 6 individual power holdings and also a retention and advancement of her power. So from 3 Times to 5 Below minus the 6 that she could have had. Let's give the power that a man possesses a power rating of **1**. The woman before the hook up has therefore 3 Times that, so that's **3**. She enters the hook up and goes **5 Down**. So that's **-5**. Then she also loses the **6 Up** she could have had if she didn't hook up, so that's **-6**. Putting these all together we get:

+3 holdings of power **-5** holdings of power **-6** holdings of power= **-8 holdings of power.** Thus we put a number on the power a woman loses if she hooks up. This is how a woman holds power. Holding the power represents "stealing the proverbial ball back," which I noted at the very end of "The Great Lie." As you can see and contrary to what the sexual liberationists have posited, for women to gain the power over men or at the very least equalise their power with men, they must do the exact opposite of what gives men power.

How does a woman gain respect? Sigmund Freud said that "life is love and work." For a woman to elicit respect from a man, she can seek it in her work life, as has happened, but she must primarily command it from her love life. As Germaine Greer insisted that women are their bodies, the woman who has an incredible career and yet uses her career aggressiveness in her sex life as a femaleist, will gain little respect from men. They may do as she orders them to do because she signs the checks, but if when out of the office or even worse *in* the office, she goes by the name Samantha, counting notches on her bed, the men secretly won't respect her. A complete double standard exists because the man who doesn't really do much except count notches on *his* bed regularly gains respect from other men, and in a sick way also from some women.

This is how a woman holds the power, this is how a woman gains respect.

57

This Instruction fulfills Box:

INSTRUCTION #3

A) The Law of Control: The more power we have in our lives, whether personally in the form of discipline and the ability to get things done or power over others, relating to our ability to influence them, the better we feel about ourselves which raises our self-esteem. A college student who took part in The Study (Part One) noted what purpose she felt the hook up served: "people have self esteem issues and think this is a way to help them by engaging in these kinds of activities…they are looking to fill that void." If we agree with Dyson's mindset of power and control existing interchangeably, we can see how Instruction #3 (holding the power) fulfills this Law. A woman who holds this strongest power has control over her life, if she has control over her life, her stress level is lower (according to Dyson) and her self-esteem higher.

C) The Law of Cause and Effect: A woman's power (cause) will give her an intangible ability to influence a man (effect).

D) The Law of Belief: A woman who believes she has great power over herself and men, necessarily *will* have great power because she believes it. A multiplier effect will take place because whether she completely understands the process or not, she not only has the power, but also believes that she has power. This alone, the belief, makes her even more powerful.

E) The Law of Expectation:

The woman who holds the power also follows the third instruction to meeting a good man. Whilst all instructions remain important, this instruction represents the cog by which all the instructions turn. Operating from a position of power has great difference to operating from a position of weakness. Instruction #3 represents a base. All around the world, people ask each other a basic question: "Where do you live?"This means, "Where is your base?" Holding the power *is* the base, it is the foundation. The successful army which ultimately wins the war, always has a strong base. If a woman can respond to the habitation question: "I arise each morning from a position of power," she has effectively positioned herself to win the war. Remember, the numbers do not add up, your quest to bag a good man is effectively a war. Power breeds confidence and confidence translates into Great Expectations.

F) The Law of Attraction: Power attracts power. A billionaire man may not have a billionaire wife, but he will have a powerful wife! There is a very good reason rich men have beautiful women by their sides, it enhances their power. A woman who can walk into a room and command attention simply by the way she looks has great power. Power attracts power. Holding the power may not bring you a billionaire, but it will bring you a powerful man in whatever realm that may be.

G) Law of Correspondence: This instruction fulfills the Law of Correspondence. If a woman holds power "within," she will hold it "without."

I) The Law of Being: This instruction fulfills this Law. If you think power, you *are* power.

H) The Law of Karma/Life's Losers: If you give power, you will receive power. The ground into which you sow power has significance. If you try to exchange power with a life loser, you look for trouble. Thankfully, you will eventually make the exchange with a good man.

All aboard...

"If women understand by emancipation the adoption of the masculine role then we are lost indeed." - Germaine Greer

INSTRUCTION FOUR

Understand You Will Meet Him,

He Will Find You!

"She turned towards the door and then suddenly Peter Harvey had dropped on one knee beside her. She looked at him wonderingly as he lifted the hem of her white muslin gown and touched his lips with it. 'Amanda,' he said, 'that is how a man, any man should approach you.'" Barbara Cartland, The Wings of Love.

INSTRUCTION FOUR

UNDERSTAND YOU WILL MEET HIM, *HE* WILL FIND YOU!

The Commitment of the Eagle

You must understand that he will find you. Oprah Winfrey and Michelle Obama hold all 39 of The Great Lie-Woman of Excellence traits and both have good men. Above and beyond their own characters, they understood this instruction, that their men should court them just as the male eagle pursues the female. A good man's commitment to you will mirror that of the male eagle, this represents one indicator of his good man status. A Woman of Excellence should expect pure courtship and nothing less. She has great worth, she has talent, a winner in life, the good man needs her, therefore she should expect a pursuit. As I began formulating this instruction with this in mind, I learned about the courtship ways of the male eagle. The male eagle leaves his nest to go and find a female. When he spots one which interests him, they then begin a game of tag. This game represents courtship. She soars high into the sky in a figure 8 pattern and makes him chase her. The male eagle no longer flies his own course, but one devised by the female (sound familiar?). After a little while, she dives to the ground finds a twig, takes it back up 10,000 feet and then drops the twig. He dives down to get it at 200 miles an hour, to catch it in mid air to take it back up to her and she responds by ignoring him (will you have the strength to do that?). At this point even though he feels very insulted he has a decision to make. Am I going to really get committed and see this through to the finish? Is this really what I want? Or should I just forget about this and maybe just find something a little easier to do with my time? She repeats this process although each time the twig gets larger and she flies at a lower altitude meaning that the twig will hit the ground faster **and he's going to have to work harder if he wants to get her.** This little game can literally go on for days. Finally she goes and gets a branch that is heavier than the eagle. She flies only 500 ft off the ground and drops it. If he catches it, they go on, if not, she flies off and **leaves him to wait for a male eagle that's got the tenacity to be her man** (did you get that?). If he's still there, it goes from courtship to commitment. She flies high to the sky and he's chasing her and suddenly she flips over onto her back, she sticks her talons up and he locks talons. At this point he's made up his mind that he's committed and he will die rather than let her go. **He continues to court her during the relationship** (a woman of excellence will accept nothing less!).

Now, I don't need to insult your intelligence by breaking this down to you. I trust you see the correlations. The courtship of a woman of excellence should never resemble, a nod, a wink and "I'm all yours," it should resemble that of the male eagle. Ladies, the good man wants an adventure to live and a beauty to fight for. To have these two, he will literally fight. You must therefore adhere to the courtship regimen right through to its completion. If a good man wants you, he will court you and every good man wants to win. "I had learned from years of experience with men, that when a man really desires a thing so deeply that he is willing to stake his entire future on a single turn of the wheel in order to get it, he is sure to win" (Thomas Edison). If women only knew how much more men needed them than women needed men, serious relationships would be in and hooking up would be out. Men need women like fish need water. According to psychological studies, marriage does have an overall positive effect on men's mental health and thus a man whether subconsciously or consciously has a vested interest in getting married. Atlanta Psychologist Frank Pitman said "marriage works for them, they have affairs because that is what they have been trained to do." Prominent government official Paul Glick estimated that "being married is about twice as advantageous to men as to women in terms of continued survival." Family sociologist Jessie Bernard confirms: "There are few findings more consistent, less equivocal (and) more convincing, than the sometimes spectacular and always impressive superiority on almost every index-demographic, psychological or social, of married over never married men. Despite all the jokes about marriage in which men indulge, all the complaints they lodge against it, it is one of the greatest boons of their sex."

When a good man shows interest, as difficult as it maybe, you have to sit back and watch him run through hula hoops, in order to get you by his side. Just as King Arthur put on his armor to fight for Guinevere, every good man wants and needs to do the same for his Queen. Only after a month of failed attempts did Barack Obama get an opportunity to entertain his law firm boss. He wooed one Michelle Robinson with "ice cream and persistence." She agreed to the pivotal meeting. "He asked me out on a date, but he invited me to one of the churches because he had been a Community Organiser and worked on the far South Side (of Chicago) with a group of churches and to see him transform himself from a guy who was a summer associate in the law firm with a suit and then to come into this church basement with folks who were like me, who grew up like me, who were challenged and struggling in ways that I never...people connected with his message and I knew that there was something different about this guy." Interviewer: "Were you smitten?" "I thought I could hang out with this guy." Do you remember the scene from the movie E.T., where the boy flies across the moon on his bike? "...we sat out on the kerb and ate ice cream cones and then I kissed her and that's when I sealed the deal." No doubt after Barack Obama 'sealed the deal' and opened Michelle's heart, he was that boy who had the energy to go through a troop and leap over a wall. Ladies-in-waiting, you have to understand that a good man, not only looks for a woman of excellence, but he needs her to fulfill his potential. As a Princeton and Harvard Law school graduate, described by Oprah as "The Real Thing," First Lady Michelle Obama is the professionals' professional and as onlookers often tell her husband: "I think the world of you Barack...but your wife!" From the 39 woman of excellence definitions in Part One, I stated that a woman of excellence can be found in three places; solely at home, as a mother, in the workplace as a career woman or at home and at work, juggling both career and family. A man in tune with what lies within him (his soul) can recognise and see past what exists on the outside of a woman, in the same way the spirit of a man can draw in a woman. When this happens, as Gertrude Stein said of Picasso, a woman *knows*: "There was nothing especially attractive about him at first sight, but his radiance, an inner fire one sensed in him, gave him a sort of a magnetism I was unable to resist." There exists a knowing, a frequency and every woman who follows the instructions can meet this man. Good men who want serious relationships exist. They live in tune with their inner world. They know what they want in a wife and when what a man pines for (the inner world of the woman) meets with a woman who has followed The Instructions, that man will do whatever he has to do in order to have the woman by his side. "With that, I want to dance with the one who brung me, the love of my life, who does everything I do, except backwards and in heels. The First Lady of the United States, Michelle Obama."

Every woman, I believe, in these 2000s needs to loosely wear the title of feminist, for if she doesn't, she will not get all she can from either her personal or career life. In the personal, the feminist woman of excellence will only accept courtship because she understands that the truly good man, confident in his abilities, will scour the earth, pulling out all the stops to find and secure a stabilized feminist force on the earth. He wants and needs this woman -"a modern day Frances Willard-typa woman who excels in her career, embraces her womanliness and would enjoy the pitter-patter of infant feet in (her) home, one day, if and only if The Right Man comes along."[8] A man needs and wants a woman who he had to chase, court, win. Women have won many victories and the incredible increase in the competent female managing directors of thriving corporations testifies to the greatness that has always existed in you. Whilst many women would accept that their assertiveness and confidence has helped them break through the glass ceilings and stay in those boardrooms as opposed to heading through the revolving doors, many would admit that the same sort of "fire" hasn't helped them in their romantic relationships. Every good man wants the last victory of approaching a woman and asking whether he can get to know her. If a woman goes after the man, she immediately emasculates him. As Germaine Greer so eloquently put it, "if women understand by emancipation the adoption of the masculine role then we are lost indeed." Good men like strong women, but not to the point of emasculation. A suitor must write letters, send flowers, *woo* a woman (at least email!!). A man needs a woman he can protect. Contrary to belief the good man wants and needs a woman who will say, "If you cramp my style and don't add to my life, I *will* tell you to pack your bags." A woman who will not have to go through the "relationship terrorism" malarkey that occurs with men who some how feel emasculated because their significant others earn as much or more than them. The good man knows the situation. Strong man, stronger woman. Ladies-in-waiting, you have to understand that men not only need good women, they desire and want a great woman. I've got to believe that President Obama had presidential aspirations years ago. It beggars belief that one day in a basketball pick up game, he made five jump shots in a row, shook his fist and declared to the world, "I'm running for President!" No doubt he knew early on about his run to The White House. Legend has it, according to his kindergarten teacher Lis Darmawan, that a "tall and curly haired child (with) sharp math skills, wrote an essay titled, "I Want To Become President." Apparently Barack Obama knew about Instruction #1 whilst still in the womb!

Assuredly also, whether subconsciously or openly by the love his mother gave him, he also knew that in order to make his journey he would need a woman like Michelle Robinson. The thinking man's thinker and ever the learner, he had to have seen that down the chain of history, the majority of successful presidents had a devoted love at their sides. The pages of history remain filled with records of great leaders whose achievements may be traced directly to the influence of women who aroused the creative faculties of their minds. Abraham Lincoln achieved greatness through the discovery and use of his faculty of creative imagination and sex desire. He discovered and began to use a faculty of creative imagination as the result of the stimulation of love, which he experienced after he met Anne Rutledge. Napoleon Bonaparte gained inspiration from his first wife, Josephine. He did well, but he later put her "aside" and when he did, he began to decline. His defeat and St Helena soon followed. "Think and Grow Rich" states: "if good taste would permit, we might easily mention scores of well-known men who climbed to great heights of achievement under the stimulating influence of their wives, only to drop back to destruction after money and power went to their heads, and they put aside the old wife for a new one. Napoleon, as not the only man to discover the sex influence, from the right source, is more powerful than any substitute of expediency which may be created by mere reason." Donald Trump understands this notion and admits his proclivity for romance. "If there isn't any romance in my life, then I don't have much incentive to be the best that I can be. That's one reason I love women. They're great motivators. I think any honest man would agree. Romantic pursuits should motivate you to be the best, to keep growing and learning. They should be the basis from which you make a lot of decisions in life...I have been with Melania for five years, and they have been **the best five years of my life**, not only personally but in business. So I figured I'd better marry the woman who stood behind me (and in front of me) during this amazing and crazy period-fast." Ladies, the good man needs you. He may not have billions, and he may not hold The Office of the President, but if he's a good man, he needs you. Most men whether consciously or subconsciously know women have great intuitive abilities which goes hand in hand with wisdom. The good man understands that a woman's words will have great sweetness the better he treats her. If a woman's words remain sweet, so will her feelings follow and if her feelings soar, her innate wisdom will also rise to astonishing levels. If a woman's wisdom rises high, her direction will also have great decisiveness and accuracy. If her direction has accuracy, a man just needs to do one thing in order to make the right decisions and have even greater success. You guessed it: follow *her* cottin' pickin' instructions! When Michelle Obama admitted that she had erred on the turnout for Senator Obama's presidential announcement in Springfield, Illinois, informing the audience 'that was the first time in a longtime I had been wrong.' The audience laughed, but for those of us who deal in truth, we know that Michelle Obama did not joke when she said this. If Christine King, the first female CEO of a semi-conductor company can say "yay" or "nay" to the potential success of a *science* project without even writing down any formulas or doing any statistical probabilities and be right 98% of the time; how correct will the intuitive woman be in social settings? Oh for a permanent Christine King, Michelle Obama, Oprah, Germaine Greer, Diane Sawyer, Katie Couric, Barbara Walters, Maria Shriver-type in my life, these years past at crucial points. I can reel them off can't I? Women naturally direct and these women direct as a vocation. All a man need do is wake up and his day would be taken care of! I do look forward to The Aisle. Any man elevates to much more when a "gravitassed" woman sits in on every scene. I've made a lot of mistakes. Decision-making represents the number one endeavor in any life. I eagerly look forward to the day when I will have no more decisions to make except whether to lift weights or not lift weights. I chuckled when Barack Obama apparently told reporters that he very much valued his wife's input and that Michelle Obama was "often" the decision-maker in the home. I am not sure if that word "often" represented inaccurate reporting or whether Barack Obama voluntarily went into the museum of his mind to recall his feelings when, unlike Bill Clinton, he actually *did* inhale. Only a man looking to regularly sleep in the spare room would say that his wife "often" made the decisions. On a personal note, I know even better days stand before me. When I say "I do," I acknowledge that my life fun really begins, but I also understand that I am making the shortest concession speech known to mankind. In preparation, I am slowly convincing myself that self-determination is overrated. Not since my mother passed, have I had a woman tell me what to do, without hesitation, with all constancy and with such a promise of severe recompense for non-compliance. I've missed that!

In conclusion, there remains no need to continuously flick your hair, smile like a Cheshire cat or click clack your heels, as you go on self-assigned catwalks across the office to see if a certain man looks at you. In football, you know how a quarterback needs a wide receiver to throw to? Dick Enberg or Al Michaels, as they commentated for the World Champion San Francisco 49ers, would repeatedly say, "And Joe Montana always seems to **find** Jerry Rice." Well ladies, so does the good man always seem to find a woman of excellence. You will meet him. He will find you. Who has the most influence? The queen who comes down off her throne to inquire whether a man has interest in her or the woman who sips wine and waits until a would-be suitor approaches her. If he approaches, she's got some decisions to make, if he doesn't, she can continue sipping her wine. The good man will find you because he needs you. If he will find you, this obviously means that you should have to get ready and expect to meet him. This doesn't mean look over your shoulder at every man who looks at you, but it does mean that you should not faint or run away when he eventually approaches you and says, "Hi."

EXPECT TO MEET HIM

How can you go about your life and career freely and yet expect a Knight's arrival? This represents probably your biggest challenge because you will inevitably have to battle loneliness. When this happens, you have to remind yourself that loneliness indicates not the absence of affection, but the absence of direction. "I started work early and came home late and there wasn't time for it." You must embrace busyness. Do general managers or managing directors promote people who wait around? How then can you expect promotion from an obliging Universe of Supreme Order to promote you if you sit around? Michelle Robinson was "busy" getting on with her life, putting her Princeton undergraduate and Harvard Law School brain to good use when suddenly an upstart Harvard law student named Barack Obama walked into her office. Stay busy, get focused on your life, but simultaneously understand there exists no point doing all this preparation and then behaving like nothing will happen. It *will* happen and right on time. The Law of Expectation states that whatever we expect with confidence becomes our self-fulfilling prophecy. Therefore we can "expect" our way to success, if you will. When a woman has prepared herself for a good man, he will appear! I've heard people say that a partner will walk into their life when they're not looking. Very true. If we understand that he will find you, it means that you have no reason to look: he has that job! A looking woman loses her edge. You do need to have your eyes open: eyes open means expectation. When he shows up, naturally you smile, you feel good, recognise the situation and move forward. Do not give him the cold shoulder, especially if you know you probably will not see him again. If the man gathered his Cohones and made the long walk over to you, do not send him packing, particularly if you find him interesting. However, if you do know you'll see him again, you can smile, perhaps even say "I don't think so." Whatever you say must communicate to him that he may have a challenge on his hands, but he *can* win you. You are a catch, he must know this for himself. If you will see him everyday, maybe you allow him to suffer in silence a bit; it worked for Michelle Obama! I like when Barack Obama took Michelle to a meeting, took off his jacket and then launched into "one of the most eloquent speeches on the way the world was and the way it should be." Barack Obama knew he had to win his wife and win her he did.

Conversely, have no aversion to love at first sight. It happens. Have an open heart for it. Deana Martin is the woman who "started work early" and had no time for romance. In "Memories Are Made of This," Deana's girlfriend Gail "begged" her to go to a dinner on Valentine's Day. On this day, already busy in her life, she met love. "As he approached, Gail kicked me under the table and said, 'He's gorgeous!' And he certainly was...tall, dark, and handsome. Then we were introduced. From the minute I saw him, I was a gonna. His beautiful face lit up with a huge smile, and he leaned down and took my hand and I melted. I can't tell you what we ate, what we drank, or anything about the evening, except this...after dinner, he walked me to my car, and we stood under the stars on a perfect night. He held my face in his hands, looked deep into my eyes, and kissed me. Still holding me in his hands, he looked at me, as if to memorize every nuance of my face, then we kissed again. A long, intense and very passionate kiss. Then, ever so softly, he said 'We should spend the rest of our lives together.'" Now that, is love at first sight!

Success emanates from the continuous pursuit of knowledge. I have always been a repository of facts. I did go to Dartmouth, but by some of the decisions I've made in life, it would not be a stretch for you to think that I had the thickness of at least three planks. Thankfully, I've learned that what counts is applied knowledge. You must thirst for applicable knowledge. If you want a good man, you must educate yourself with what a good man would want. When you took your SAT exams, the type of questions did not surprise you did they? Very often divorces and break ups emanate from unpreparedness. The good man does not want a woman who will learn on the job. Expecting him means preparing for his arrival. Will you know how to speak? Will you have "those dinner clothes" to wear? Will you know how to say what he needs to hear? The good man's language sounds like this: "I want to be with you because I know you will make me better than I already am." Can someone say Barack Obama? Ladies, if you think for one second that President Obama got to The White House solely off his own merits, without the strength, sentimentality, intelligence, love, direction and wisdom of Michelle Obama, I suggest you put down The Pipe they accused me of smoking when I went on Temptation Island to find love. "The Closer on the Campaign Trail, the rock of the Obama family." Just as Michelle Obama did not joke about hardly ever being wrong, so was Barack Obama very serious about his words. No Michelle Obama, no Pennsylvania Avenue, it is that simple. Some arrogant men will say that it cannot be that simple. Oh, but it really is! Whilst Barack Obama's words served as an introduction, they make for an even better description of Michelle Obama. Particularly in the early stages, everything you do with a good man must inform him that you can make him better whilst you allow him to prove his worthiness to you. This all takes study, thought, action, reflection, contemplation, all of which you will receive motivation to do when you really expect his arrival. Do you see how expecting his arrival entails much more than just a gleeful feeling?

Remember, expecting to meet him means keeping busy with your life focus and direction. You must not, however, build a fortress around yourself. It remains understandable why you will attempt to hide. Past pain and the fact that the record number of children attributed to one man is 899 both explain your actions. Understand that when the good man arrives, you must have an ability to get out from behind any constructed wall as soon as you "detect" his good man status. Remember, good men have many applicants. There exists a difference between having a wall up and letting a man chase you and fight to peel you like an orange. If he wants to peel you, it means that he believes the sweetness that lies within warrants his pursuit. Barack Obama used ice cream to make his case. Whatever food your suitor uses, he must make his case. He must court you, but you must understand what transpires before your eyes and engage yourself in the purposeful, deliberate and the gradual unveiling of yourself.

This Instruction fulfills Box:

<u>INSTRUCTION #4</u>

A) The Law of Control: You have control of the situation by actually waiting and allowing it to develop. The idea that you have control by sitting back may appear confusing, but you must understand that you are not just sitting back, you actually exercise great proactiveness. Your esteem will grow as a result because you know the process.

B) The Law of Expectations: With confidence, you expect for him to find you.

C) The Law of Belief: The fact that you not only believe, but actually know the good man needs you, should allow you to also believe with confidence that he is on his way.

D) The Law of Correspondence: Your understanding of this instruction will give you great peace and this will show through.

E) The Law of Human Destiny: the knowledge that he will find you (cause) should give you a strong sense of comfort that your future is clear (effect).

"I want someone to come and stay and be there because he wants to, not because he has a piece of paper that says he has to." - Halle Berry

INSTRUCTION FIVE

Know Good Man Definition/

Use Intuition

INSTRUCTION FIVE
KNOW GOOD MAN DEFINITION/USE INTUITION

A good man is a man who wants to walk side by side with a woman of his choosing, primarily because of how he "feels" when he thinks of her in a non-sexual way. He appreciates her so much that he wants to protect her emotionally and physically. Sure he finds her desirable and attractive, but he values her company as much as he values his own and generally more. What is a good man? Well, I want to go on record as saying that you will not necessarily meet a good man in Church. God remains faithful, the Torah rejuvenates, the Bible reads Holy and prayer changes things, this all remains irrefutable; but if you think just because a man goes to Church on Sunday, can say Amen on Q and can recite the Our Father without hesitation, that his arrival on your scene equates to The Second Coming of Jesus Christ, then I suggest that you once again put down The Pipe. Good men derive from all faiths, religions and backgrounds. I will say this though, if the man goes to a Synagogue and derives from the Jewish faith, then you've entered a different standard. The consistency I've seen amongst Jewish people, I have not found elsewhere in my life. But this represents another discussion. The point here remains that the Church far from has exclusivity on good men, as a matter of fact some of the most despicable men and women who exist on earth, sit front row at The Higher Life Receive Jesus Today Center, singing Alleluia to the King. Gandhi did say, "I like your Christ, I do not like your Christians. They are so unlike your Christ." Remember ladies, goodness does not appear in specific labels. A good man derives from any faith; that would be your faith, mine and everybody else's. You must look at his intention, his heart. A profound scripture reads, "Blessed are the pure in heart, for they shall see God." Remember that!

When bank tellers undergo training, they handle large amounts of real money so that they get a strong "feel" for authenticity, thus when counterfeit money crosses their hands they know immediately.

As a woman of excellence or burgeoning woman of excellence who has decided to embark on this second express train, it remains vitally important for you to have met, read about and perhaps even studied many good men of character so that when a pretender dials your number, you will know immediately. Immediately is the operative word here. You do not have time to go for five and six year sojourns with men who will turn around and say that they're just not ready to settle down. It surprises me, the number of women who continue to get their hearts broken especially with all the emotional intelligence they have always possessed. I can tell a man's intentions towards a woman in about five seconds, so it pains me when I hear all these women who waste their young years away, jumping in and out of long relationships. I can't be everywhere, that's why I'm making this second journey with you.

So ladies, identify successful marriages and relationships in your life and find a way to hang around these couples, so you will have a working idea of what it should look like and most importantly how the man operates. We all typically remain the same and revert back to type as we get older. A man just doesn't meet a woman and completely change. To the contrary, he will just become more of who he already is. If he had great successes before you, they will continue with you in his life. If the man had women on the go before he met you, guess what? If he had an anger problem before he met you, it will continue? If he cheated on women before he met you, it's in his blood? You know where I am going with this, leopards and spots? With this then, when you talk to a potential mate, question yourself not so much about his looks, smile or wallet, but moreso his character. Once or twice in my life, a woman did not find my character enough, she wanted first to see my wallet before going any further. Because I was a poor college graduate, I couldn't impress them with thousands of dollars and so I forfeited the right to take them out *even once*. I know one man who obviously had a better ground game than me because *he* pulled it off:

Michelle Obama: I visited (the Washington DC Apartment) but I didn't sleep there. I saw it long enough to know that I wasn't going to stay there…it reminded me of a little version of the apartment you were in when we first started dating…that was a dump too!

Barack Obama: That was when I had the car with the hole in it?

Michelle Obama: You could see the sidewalk because of the rust had gone through, so that was my side. I would look and see the ground pass…and I still married him!

Barack Obama: That's how I knew she loved me, it wasn't for my money[9]

Many a woman loses out because she views a man superficially first. Sure, you want to live comfortably, what woman doesn't? However, it behooves you significantly to assess as quickly as possible: does this man have character? Does he resemble those men I've viewed in successful relationships? Imagine if Michelle Obama had turned her nose up as so many women do? She would have regretted it for the rest of her life. In Part One, I compared men to apples by saying that once you bite into a man, it's the same taste through and through. In order to have a good man by your side, who will stay "because he wants to," it remains imperative that you know what he looks like, smells like, breathes and thinks like. Knowing the good in order to spot the bad and certainly not the other way around. A woman's ability to spot the bad, clouds her thinking, makes her overly pessimistic and unable to spot a good man when he arrives on the scene. If you follow the instructions, he; they, will arrive. Understand though that the good man, although understanding, does not want to spend weeks, months and even years proving himself. He will understand the caution, but after a while if you do not get "hip" to his authenticity and difference from the others, he will walk away and especially today, where beautiful women abound and men remain in the minority. A good man doesn't have to wait around. You have to find a way to discern his intentions: words and actions over a period of time usually make for the best indicators, although many individuals have an ability to discern a person's intentions immediately and accurately. You do not have the time to entertain all new recruits. You must assess quickly and move on. Do not solicit third party reports, a best friend's opinion, a business associate, mother, sister or allow anyone to assess a situation for you, ultimately you will live with the man, not them. Additionally, there could be 1001 reasons why they will give you wrong information. Hear him on the phone, look him in the eye and make your own judgement. Know the real dollar bills! Until you do, you will endure drama after drama. Many a woman has lost a good man, because someone told them something, their emotional minds went into overdrive and instead of investigating, they ran to the closest man who held his arms open and offered a ring. Time to say Au Revoir to these testing times by doing your homework. If you want a man to stay, you're gonna have to know all about The Few Good Men and less about The Players, as opposed to all about The Players and very little about The Few Good Men. Those women who say they want a good man and yet have not spent time studying what he looks or sounds like, delude themselves! We do live in tough times, women experience great difficulty meeting good men, but they exist and they number more than you can imagine. And besides, you only need one!

THE GOOD MAN

On my travels, I watched and studied men of character in order to give me a working definition of a good man. From managers to coaches to teammates to Presidents to doctors to lawyers to CEOs, what follows is what I found most consistently:

1) A good man has a job or a life work. Whether he stays at home, in a little role reversal to the norm, and the woman of his life works out of the home, his familial goal and life work lies in fostering an environment for the woman of his life to excel. A good man is a man of quality and "a man of quality is never intimidated by a woman of equality." He recognises that he has an equal at his side. In other words, you should never feel that you have to shrink in his presence. He should encourage you to be more. In his presence, you increase. As John Lennon sang, "Imagine." I ask you to imagine the feeling of growing and filling up with joy emotion when you remain in his company. This man has a sense of comfort about himself. With your women's intuition firmly in tune, you will know when a good man approaches you. Something he writes, something he says, should literally scream at you. Once again, we do live in tough times and your number one challenge will be determining Riff from Raff. With your intuition in tact, if his words speak to you, go with it, but you have to have wholeness to ensure that you simply do not hear what you want to hear. He will have a presence.

2) A good man is consistent. He lives by the common adage: "What we are by letters when absent such persons we are by deed when present." Most women can testify to the fact that when they've dated a man long enough, they eventually realise that they are spending their time with at least two people! We all have different aspects to our characters, but if one side of the man you have met runs smooth, while with the other side, he resembles those sociopaths we hear about on the news from time to time, he gives you very concentrated information. A good man is the same front stage before people, as he is back stage at home. "The secret to Ronald Reagan is that there is no secret. He is exactly the man he appears to be. The Ronald Reagan you see in public is the same Ronald Reagan I live with...There aren't any dark corners to Ronald Reagan's character that will be revealed twenty years from now, no desperate moments of anguish, indecision, and self-doubt. Of course he has his moods and his disappointments, but on the whole, Ronnie is the most upbeat man I've ever known."[10] This kind of man has a consistency to his character that should both calm and reassure you. When a woman meets this man, she will witness a stable authenticity and not a rendition, profile or showcase theater.

3) A good man is a finished product and not a WIP (Work In Progress). A grandfather once said: "They used to make ships of wood and men of steel, but now they make ships of steel and men of wood." A good man is a man of steel. This means you will not have to carve him out from the woodwork or ore him, like a diamond miner, because he will enter your life unraveled and complete. He may come from the projects or the Hamptons; it really does not matter, but the condition in which he arrives has the significance. Because he arrives as a finished product, he should have had successes along the way. He just knows he can do and be more. *You* grow in his presence and *he* needs you for expansion, it remains practically a done deal! Listen to the man carefully when he tells you about his life. A man who has had a train wreck life with no direction and just a string of 28 years of bad luck, gives you concentrated information. A woman of excellence will provide extra direction, needed comfort, assured focus, but if a man hasn't found a railway line in 28 years, even Mother Theresa would have admitted that you have a job on your hands. Understand though, you should not start hallucinating, believing that the man isn't exactly as you would like him to be; but by the power vested in you; you can mold and rebuild him. You are not The Artist formerly known as Prince, neither are you Michelangelo or Picasso. Rather than trying to make The Revolution, just acknowledge that social workers earn their keep before authorities section individuals under The Mental Health Act. Not your job. You *can* help him be more, but you *will* push up the daisies early on your grave, if you try to make a man different than who he already is in his natural state. Whatever you meet on Day One will equate to what you will have after three kids. It therefore benefits you greatly to descend from the clouds after you have met him and examine him early, quickly and meticulously. Could I live with this? How do I feel in his presence? Can I make him more? Will he make me grow? It's very easy. Men reveal themselves immediately, you just have decisions to make. Listen to the man keenly, every sentence will give you more concentrated information. As you can tell, I like the concept of concentrated information. If you try to take on a project or a flawed character by denying the blatantly obvious, you could be the one out of two women who dies from heart disease. In 1995, 41% of the women who died, died of heart disease. Heart disease remains the number one killer of women, killing ten times more women than breast cancer and all the other cancers combined. Mark my words, if you take on a Project Flaw, he will eventually make you uneasy and he *will* break your heart!!

4) A good man enjoys healthy competition. He likes to win. He wants to be the best at what he does. If a man has a blasé attitude towards life, not really bothered whether he succeeds or not, then he gives you more concentrated information.

5) A good man is faithful. He has decided to love with purpose, intentionality, sacrifice, sensitivity, and therefore with a greater intensity. He lives by Semper Fidelis: Always Faithful. He will not visit Yankee Stadium to see what he can bat, frequenting the bars and the clubs with the drink and the Saturday Night Fever disco lights because he has all he wants in his life: you. If a man still wants to spend Boys' Nights out and view other women, once you are an item, then you know what I am going to say? A good man doesn't care how many women he can potentially bed, he flees and stays away from slippery places because he understands the Danish proverb: "He that does not want to fall ought not to stand in slippery places." And so he monitors himself, so he won't do anything behind his woman's back which she would not appreciate him doing in her presence. It's been said that "it's not the first look at the girl's legs that's the problem, it's the second." A good man has eyes, but he doesn't need to check if they work with every woman which passes by.

6) A good man is a man of his word. The Jewish marriage tradition summates the nature of the bond between a good man and a woman: king and queen. The "kallah" will sit on a "throne" to receive her guests, while guests surround the "chatan" to toast him.

Traditionally, the mother of the bride and the mother of the groom stand together and break a plate. This symbolically shows the seriousness of the commitment - just as a plate can never be fully repaired, so too a broken relationship can never be fully repaired. Just as you make a personal contract with yourself about not coming out of The Instructions until you get what you want, the chatan and kallah make a together-forever agreement.

7) A good man doesn't necessarily go to church, but does usually believe in prayer. And if he doesn't, by the time he's hung out with you for a few weeks, he *will!* "Prayer and action are needed to uphold the sanctity of human life, I believe it will not be possible to accomplish our work without being a soul of prayer"(Ronald Reagan).

8) A good man will ensure that the woman of his life eats well everytime he sits at the table with her. She will also have a "Huh" feeling everytime the phone rings, whether three dates or three years have passed. If you do not enjoy your meal more with the good man around, then skip him, he's not your man. "We were just so happy together and so very comfortable in each other's company. We talked and laughed easily together, just as we had ever since our first date. We both quickly saw that we both wanted to live the same way and liked to do the same things."[11]

9) A good man may love people, but remains very particular about who he lets close to him. Differential Association Theory signifies the concept of "me mates." 'Me Mates' equates to The Brat Pack, the main reason for betrayals. With whom a man spends time can give you as much information as anything the man could ever verbalise. He may call himself a one woman man, but if he hangs out with Hugh Heffner? Even if a guy has values and integrity, even if you think he sounds like the quintessential good man, if he communes with louts, he will steer toward loutadom, slowly: "Although he loves people, he often seems remote, and he doesn't let anybody close. There's a wall around him. He lets me come closer than anyone else, but there are times when even I feel the barrier…Ronnie is an affable and gregarious man who enjoys other people, but unlike most of us, he doesn't need them for companionship or approval."[12]

10) A good man will express his feelings to the woman by his side.

"Man can't live without a heart and you are my heart, by far the nicest thing about me and so very necessary. There would be no life without you nor would I want any."[13]

"How come you moved in on me like this? I'm hollow without you and 'hollow' hurts"[14] (Ronald Reagan).

11) A good man uses anger for his benefit. It serves him, he does not succumb to anger. Anger has a place. When you see where a man puts his anger, you see the man. Correct anger is passion, drive. Contrary to belief, it is extremely necessary for accomplishment and change. Just like sex emotion, correctly channeled anger can elevate a person to iconic status. It should represent a foundation for change, not a vehicle to air and vent personal issues. Anger has power and can motivate masses. Motivation equates to nothing but anger that has found an appropriate place. Constructive anger builds, destructive anger kills. Destructive anger says, "Things are not going my way so I am going to take it out on you." Constructive anger says: "How many times did I give you that instruction?" The man who doesn't get angry, doesn't get to much in life. Sometimes things do not happen until a voice is raised: "The Presidency maybe the most pressured job in the world but Ronnie didn't get grumpy or yell at his staff. It takes a lot to make him angry, although now and then he does lose his temper. When it happened in the Oval Office, he would take off his glasses and throw them on the desk. I never actually witnessed this, but apparently that was a signal-when the glasses go down, stand back."[15]

12) A good man has a sense of humor. From hearing him for just minutes, you will know that if you were to ever marry, he would respect you and his mother-in-law. At the same time, ever the joker, he would keep a good opener in his pocket. Nancy Reagan commented on her husband: "Later Ronnie's only complaint about Mother was that she had ruined one of his favorite jokes. For years, he liked to open his speeches by telling his audience, 'I face you with mixed emotions.' Then he would define 'mixed emotions' as the feelings a man has as he watches his mother-in-law drive over the cliff in his new Cadillac."[16]

LIVE BY WOMEN'S INTUITION

"There's a part of me that I didn't even know I had until recently- instinct, intuition, whatever. It helps me and protects me. It's perceptive and astute. I just listen to the inside of me and I know what to do"[17] (Inez, thirty-year-old mother of three).

Women of excellence, you have a gift. You've had it since birth. Physicians and physiologists have used magnetic resonance imaging and PET scans to examine the functioning of the brain in detail. They found that under stimulation, men and women's brains lit up in different areas, thus confirming that their brains were different. This accounts for the difference in behaviors and attitudes between men and women. A discussion of these differences should therefore not raise eyebrows or brand anyone as sexist: scientists have proven these differences. Men and women see things differently because of the way their brains operate: a woman's corpus callosum will transmit electrical signals better than it will for men due to the testosterone bath which baby boys experience from six and seven weeks old. Please do not turn off your gift because you've sat alone with Cuddles the terrier for three years and you see a man who "looks good." Contingent upon knowing the good man definition rests the firm fact that you must "detect" him as soon as he approaches you. Wanting to placate your ego and its delusional vetting processes, you pray about your situation, and receive confirmation, "He'll do." You get up off your knees and you marry the guy. It shocks me at the number of women who get tricked, conned and played day after day. Every interaction with a man will just be variations of what you witnessed when you first met him. Many a woman has lost a good man because they neglected their own gift. Many a woman has gained ulcers because she refused to listen to her gift. "I learned that when you see a flag in a relationship; next time, recognise it as a flag and not just a shadow; it's a flag"(Halle Berry). Ladies, if I can tell a potential cheater-cheater pumpkin eater in seconds and that's after getting little sleep the night before, I know you can pick one out after spending an evening with him! I know that women often do ridiculous things like, "If I'm really meant to be with him, I'll push him away, if he's still around, then he's a keeper." For an emotionally and intellectually rich sex, this seems dumber than Laurel and Hardy at their best. This backward thinking explains how some women have missed good men. Listen to your gift, go with your gift.

This Instruction fulfills Box:

INSTRUCTION #5

A) The Law of Expectation

B) The Iron Law of Human Destiny, the Law of Cause & Effect simply states that everything happens for a reason. Your knowledge of a good man (cause) will mean that you will have the ability to eliminate "okay" men (effect) very easily. This will direct your life path.

C) The Law of Control: By knowing the good man, you take control of your love life because you will know what to look for when he approaches. Having this control, according to Law, thus gives you self-esteem.

D) The Law of Correspondence: Your knowledge of a good man will affect how you operate on the outside. You will have a level of comfort with men right from the outset because you "know" the traits of a good man.

"*Intent is a force that exists in the universe. When sorcerers (those who live of the Source) beckon intent, it comes to them and sets up the path for attainment, which means that sorcerers always accomplish what they set out to do.*"
- Carlos Castaneda

INSTRUCTION SIX

Sharpen

The Saw

"*We are not human beings having a spiritual experience. We are spiritual beings having a human experience.*"- Pierre Teilhard de Chardin

INSTRUCTION SIX
SHARPEN THE SAW

Once you become comfortable with the fact that the man you want will find you, your job now entails making yourself the very woman, the exact kind of man you want will pursue. This takes personal honesty. You have to reach a point where you can admit to yourself, that if the type of man you want hasn't found you, you still have some work to do. Either that or just become resigned to settling for what does approach you. The truth remains that you may not have much work to attract the caliber of man you want. When you consider the difference between a world record holder and another talented athlete could lay simply in the warm up routine or the amount of rest two days before the race, it remains easy to understand how tweaking your regimen could also bring phenomenal results. The thought of you remaining single or meeting the man of your dreams should inspire you to self-examination. Plato said that the unexamined life was not worth living. You have to examine, investigate and do due diligence on *every* facet of your life from what and how much you read to what you wear and when you wear it. Deep investigation might reveal that you have a lot of work to do, but if you want a good man, you'll do it.

Sharpening The Saw, a term invented by Stephen Covey, represents a commitment to increase a product's potential in order to achieve a greater output. Economists call it investing or priming the pump. In the case of attracting a good man, this means having more influence mentally, physically, socially and spiritually and you can only get more influence in these areas by working on them. Kaizen, the Japanese concept of continuous improvement, represents this idea. You function better when you constantly work on the main sectors of your life and to have the good man by your side, you have to be your best. As I mentioned early, times have changed and you delude yourself if you believe the acquisition of a good man as nothing other than a competitive sport. The only difference lies in the fact that you compete against yourself.

Mental Sharpening

How do you work out mentally? Frances Bacon said that reading makes a person "full." He had no reason to lie. In order to work out mentally, you simply just have to read. Romance novels do count, but the average man needs to talk about something other than Mills and Boone! Reading allows you to engage in the life of others. It widens your mind and keeps you alert. The good man needs a woman who can and will listen to him, as he pours out things he ordinarily would have to keep to himself as a single. Staying sharp can only heighten your understanding and knowledge, both of which you'll need as you play the psychiatrist role in your relationship! At some point of the day, women will express their emotions (normally to another woman) by "getting it out" of their system. In this way, they make their emotions work for them positively because once they have aired what sits in their minds, they feel "cleansed" and ready to move on. This alone confirms why women as a whole enjoy better mental health than men. Many men air their issues by reaching for the gun. Women reach for the phone. Women typically listen exceptionally well and listening necessitates a strong psychological element which involves engagement. The quicker you engage a man and enter into his inner dialogue without even speaking, the quicker you get to his heart. As you know, you get to his heart, you get him! This engagement requires mental sharpness. The difference between a mentally, intellectually full woman and one who does not have this, equates to the difference between having internet service and not having an internet service - a world. Understand that I do not refer to quickness. From the thousands of women I have met in my life, I have not met one who couldn't out sprint a lion when it comes to a response. I believe the slowest woman on earth could respond intelligently to a brick wall! A woman has this gift. But here with this particular sharpening, I refer to intelligence, discourse, subject matter and title, not a comeback.

Typically, as a woman, you will have an ability to express yourself, you must use this gift, not to mock or ridicule a man ever, but always to build him up. The right words spoken at the right time can have a man loving you forever. Conversely, the wrong words spoken at the wrong time can have him running in the opposite direction and into another bed. I emphasise to you that after the initial attraction your mind and words will draw him in and keep him. When a woman has a sharpened intelligence, her thoughts vibrate at a different frequency and as we know, this ushers in the desired object by allowing the Law of Attraction to work positively.

Physical Sharpening

You have to work on your bodies. I've heard some single women say that they do not like to workout. I always respond in the same way, "Well, you must not like men then!" Visually stimulated, your body and looks will attract a man, your vibration will keep him around, your heart will close the deal. But in order to close the deal, you have to get his attention first and your body and looks perform that function. A man cannot "bypass" your body and head straight for your mind. No matter how good you are, if you cannot first get the man to look at you because of the way you look, he *will* look right past you. A woman should exercise anyway, but the woman who does not work out and yet expects to meet a good man, positively lives a pipe dream. Many women have resorted to plastic surgery to get their looks and body in order. But, as one patient said, "the effects are short-lived, the risks significant and there are no guarantees." Dr Michael Prager, a plastic surgeon in London's Wimpole Street commented, "four out of five clients regret their decision to have anti-ageing surgical pro-cedures...the truth is you can't improve the state of healthy skin by cutting it." Plastic surgery does not provide the answer. You do not need to be a model, but you should look healthy. The old fashioned salty sweat remains the order of the day. Working out, aerobic activ-ity, releases endorphins which relieve pain, reduce stress, enhance the immune system and postpone the aging process. Moreso than attempting to stay looking young, working out enables you to look your best which several decades ago may not have been entirely necessary. A healthy woman glows and remains very recognisable to the eye. Just be healthy. Your look will attract him initially. The contradiction becomes apparent when you acknowledge that your heart and words will keep him, not your body. You attract him physically and win him emotionally, not with an emotional mess, because you've dealt with that and become whole, but with your emotional availability. Whether you practice yoga, do Pilates, run, lift weights, play basketball, do high powered walking, whatever you choose to do, it remains vitally important that you stay healthy. Working out only brings benefits. Moreso than body conscious, you need to be health conscious. Ladies, don't try and re-invent the wheel, just work out. No plastic surgery or diet pills, just good old fashioned salt...it does a body good!

Social Sharpening

This doesn't mean party, although dinner parties, girls' movie nights, girls' chat fest sessions represent great ideas. Social sawing means get out of your comfort zone to meet people unlike you. What makes others tick? Most important is not the label you hold and carry, it's who you are and what you represent. Most people call this socialising, making friends. However, you as a woman have to make friends because you are not waiting to be found but *preparing* yourself to be found. For this you need to move in circles. Once in a while, a good man will knock on your door and want to sell you something, but with the internet and telephone, personal cold calls do not have as much popularity. I believe a woman should go out and about, busying herself with her life. Why? The numbers. A man can take a walk at anytime of the day, pass by a woman on his way and say, "Can I get your number?" A woman can't do this with any degree of long-lasting success.

Spiritual Sharpening

Every facet of The Saw thus far will benefit you immensely. Individually beneficial, they all work together in order to maximise this final sharpening. This Saw represents "The Closer" with this closer presentation, if you will. I've met some of the most beautiful women in the world, some of the most intelligent women in the world and some of the fittest women in the world. Daily, as a model, former basketball player and Ivy man, I give thanks to the Lord Our God for the life chances bestowed upon me: me, the peanut and chicken-eating, book worm, born in one Dulwich Village, London. But for all the beauty, athleticism and brains I have seen in women across the world, the spiritual woman is more to be desired than fine gold. The woman of spirit is more than enough, but if a woman happens to have any one or a combination of the three: beauty, athleticism and brains, in conjunction with spirituality, this woman will literally need bodyguards! Since the world has both a physical and spiritual component, we are also all spiritual beings. This means that there do exist spiritual mates for you, they just have to find you and you just have to meet them. Tapping into the spiritual realm just helps the process along. If you are single and not tapping into the spiritual realm, you diminish your opportunities to meet your mate by at least 85%. You lower your MAG (Mate Attracting Geiger). I did not arrive at this percentage scientifically, I actually think that the woman who doesn't tap into her spiritual dimension (saw) minimalises all her career and personal life chances, because this realm will give you direction and location. Just how I respond to the woman who doesn't work out, I respond in the same way to the woman who doesn't pray. The minimilisation occurs due to our spirit nature. In effect, you already have a connection to what and to whom you want in your life by the human spirit and by The Universe. We are all here just paying rent under the same huge roof! No human being could manufacture an individual of cells with such a capacity for self-preservation, mental, physical and social. No human being could devise the intricate process of childbirth with a woman having a fetus as small as the smallest little finger nail, germinate into a living, breathing vessel after nine months. You have to pray. MC Hammer sang, "I say we pray just to make it today."

Personally, I say you should pray just to make sure your good man walks your way! When you ask the Universe and The Meticulous Being of Order for a future, in this case a good man, you will have severe tests, mainly because The Creator wants to see who you'll call upon in the tough times. Great lows necessarily accompany great highs. If you do not want great joys, with the best that you can possibly reach and attain, simply do not pray. If you do not pray, you will not be in the right place to meet a career advancement, but more importantly, your spiritual mate. There exist no coincidences.

To what spirit do I refer? Is it the spirit of the Hindu, Buddhist, Scientologist, Christian, Catholic, Jew? We all have spirits, the human spirit, but once we all recognise a Spirit (Source) beyond the human spirit, we set connections into motion. If we can understand that we are all connected by one Source and see the Source as the Clearinghouse if you will, it means that we can connect to others we neither see nor know, via The Source. We are but beads of sweat molecules in a river of humanity. And The Source can open the floodgates and connect whomever He wants, when He wants. Your ability to reach God, The Light, The Source, Spirit, whatever you want to call Him, depends on the condition of your heart. If you want to tap into the spiritual with a profundity of success, get your heart right. That scripture, "Blessed are the pure in heart for they shall see God," does not say blessed are the Christians or blessed are the Hindus or blessed are the Scientologists, it says if your heart is pure, you will see God. Another scripture miles away from the first one says: "Who shall ascend into the hill of the Lord?...He that has clean hands and a pure heart." Informing me about the label you wear, tells me no more about you than you informing me that you like to eat grapes. There are people who walk around with Bibles and when they pray the walls literally shake, but their hearts remain debase. Conversely, there exist those who never open a Bible, who never enter Church buildings and yet, if they do pray, things move, due to the authenticity of their prayer and the genuineness of their hearts. A pure heart, without the actual act of prayer represents a prayer in itself. Admittedly, as I mentioned,

I have had a love affair with Jewish people my whole life, but I have learned first and foremost to look at the heart of an individual because The Owner looks at the same thing. The Owner effectively says that he has already given you your hearts desire, but He wants you engaged in the attainment process because he refuses to absolve you of human responsibility. "It's yours, but you've got to ask me. It's yours but you have to take it." You have to possess it in the spirit first and then it will manifest in the natural. If you can see the dream, you can have it. If you can see the good man, you can have him too, but you've got to see him first! Certain words should never leave your minds! If you do not possess something in the spiritual first, you will not be able to handle it in the natural. You have to see yourself with a good man in order to be able to handle one in the natural. By reading these instructions, you have already agreed to "see" your good man. Why can't every woman have a good man? Two reasons: some won't follow the instructions and some have ugly hearts. For those who have ugly hearts and won't follow the instructions, there exists more hope for a serial killer on death row than for these women to meet a good man. Didn't want to put it so crassly, but you need this point. But for you who will follow the instructions and will work daily on your heart, he's on his way. Chalk It Up!!

Prayer of Agreement

The Meticulous Being Of Order is not a fool now. You have to realise that there exists power in numbers. Who has more influence? The daughter who asks her father for something or the daughter who brings her best girlfriend with her and they both ask? If you have people pray for you and pray for you without a double heart: i.e. "I pray Jane meets her good man, but let him not be too good," you're in business!! The sincerity and intensity of the person praying makes the significant difference. A scripture reads: "Again I say unto you that if two of you shall agree on earth as touching anything that they shall ask, it shall be done for them of my Father which is in heaven." Scientifically, the concept of quantum entanglement, gets closest to explaining what occurs when individuals separated by space pray for each other: "Two objects created together are entangled, send one to the other side of the Universe, now do something to one and the other responds instantly, so either information is travelling infinitely fast or in reality they are still connected and space is just the construct that gives the illusion that they are separated"(Entanglement explanation).

This Instruction fulfills Box:

INSTRUCTION #6

A) The Law of Control: Sharpening the Saw puts your life in your hands. It is a proactive instruction. You have the ability to work on yourself daily by fine tuning/developing your whole person and this means that you have control of your daily advancement. You do not wait for some outside force to dictate your schedule. Your self-esteem automatically rises with this. Do not be surprised in this period if many so-called friends start to get mad at you because they see you taking control of your life. Jealousy always raises its ugly head in times of positive change. Look at it as a purging period.

B) The Law of Belief: You will/should have confidence that your future is hidden in your daily routine and this instruction puts the burden completely on you.

C) The Law of Correspondence: Internally, body, mind and spirit you are constantly evolving. You will act consistent with this truth.

D) The Law of Expectation: You expect great things to happen by sharpening the saw. Great things do happen.

E) The Law of Attraction: Your renewed confidence in all four sectors of your person will show and you will attract what you want and sadly what you don't want. Remember light attracts moths! Sharpening the saw daily will make you so attractive that you will literally need a bodyguard!

F) The Law of Karma: Your positive vibrations will boomerang back to you. Understand here that some people are so hidden in their own world of negativity and wrong thought that a large coach dose of positivity will still have them sending negativity back. Not your concern.

G) The Law of Being: Daily, by sharpening the saw, you have an opportunity to renew your thoughts and re-affirm exactly who you are and what you are about. What you become will cause fascination on the part of others. You must not become conceited, but instead make a commitment to continue the process of daily renewal and improvement.

"There is no such thing as chance, what appears to us the merest accident springs forth from the deepest source of destiny."- Johann Federich Von Schiller

INSTRUCTION SEVEN

Show Gratitude by Connecting

Others to their Dreams

"The best way to be happy and have fulfillment is to concentrate your life on persons other than yourself. You become a better and more satisfied person while you help others to become better than they've ever been in their lives." - Sargeant Shriver

INSTRUCTION SEVEN

SHOW GRATITUDE BY CONNECTING OTHERS TO THEIR DREAMS

Unthankful people always live in squalid conditions; if not literal squalor, they exist in the squalor of their minds. If an ungrateful person has great success, they will not enjoy it. If an unthankful person has little success, the cycle of unthankfulness and failure will continue. You should have gratitude all through every day. We all endure tough and painful experiences both in our personal and career lives, but we still go on and survive to fight many more days. Everything that has happened in your life has brought you to this point and whilst you may have had tough experiences, you have grown from them and moved on. Be thankful that you have learned and moved on. No matter what circumstances we find ourselves in, good or bad, there has to exist something where we can demonstrate true gratitude. Oprah keeps a gratitude journal. She has become notorious for giving things away (Angel Network) and perhaps she can solely take responsibility for having her studio audiences search beneath their seats to find a gift. Michelle Obama constantly refers to the sacrifices her parents made in order for her to go to Princeton and then Harvard. Still, amidst all her talent and opportunity, when prompted she notes that her daughters remain her priority and made it clear to her husband that he would have to fit his schedule around them. "It's all about them." Needing to take a break from motivational speaking and Entertainment, I had the honor and privilege of working for Madeleine Kernot, the managing director of TNS Global Media Intelligence UK. I enjoyed being apart of her company so much, that I inquired if they had TNS Global jackets to wear! Completely geared for career advancement, the set up of the company fostered situations where others could achieve their dreams. She treats the company as any mother would her own baby and what mother wouldn't want the best for her baby? What mother wouldn't want her baby to achieve its dreams? With these three women of excellence, there exists almost a palpable and selfless need to "Pass It On." A mentality which says: "I'm having my fun, how about us seeing if we can get you some fun too." Ladies, did it ever occur to you that blessings keep flowing to a person when they truly show gratitude for what they already have and have conquered greed? A person who truly has gratitude for their lives, will out of an overflow, want to enable others to achieve their dreams and not hinder the progression of another. When you make something happen for another, helping them achieve their dream, you set in motion a series of vibrations which the Universe responds to by orchestrating events for your own dream fulfillment. Typically, you will receive your dream and much more. Ask any of the three women of excellence mentioned above. This is by Law. If you have true and great comfort giving away things, the Universe can trust you with abundant wealth. If you have true and great comfort as a single, the Universe can trust you with a good man. Note this. Ultimately, the progression of your immediate environment has always got to take paramount importance.

Life represents a game with certain rules. If we adhere to these rules called the Laws of the Universe, we get what we want period. Naturally there exist the automatic ups and downs which we must wade through, but once waded, we will have what we want if we stick close to the Laws of the Universe. The truth remains that if you find yourself with a gaping hole that you have not found a way to fill, truthful examination will allow you to pinpoint a Universal Law or Laws which you have not satisfied or in this case, an instruction which you have not followed. Some people play the game of life well and some people do not. The quickest way to stop the flow of goodwill into your life rests firmly in begrudging the good game players. We live in challenging times. Will you act like the cannibal, the person concerned only about your own survival or will you enter The Village mentality? People use tactics of delay and misinformation to get ahead and by doing so they write their own obituaries; by Law. If you can give something to someone, give it, you write your own future; by Law. The Law of The Farm does not just apply to the cornfields of Iowa, it also pertains to life. Ensuring he uses the right soil, a farmer plants a seed and then waits for the harvest. Life shows no difference. We must plant in the right soil in order to get desired "harvests." When we do, we reap what we sow, more than we sow and later than we sow. This is by Law. If you plant seeds of goodness, kindness and generosity where you can and in the right soil, the Universe, set up by a Divine and Meticulous Being of Order, has to comply. This is by Law. Do you get the feeling I want to impress on you a certain exactness by reiterating the golden words, "by Law"? You feel correctly. Whether career or personal, if you have an opportunity to help somebody else, do so, you only help yourself. Having said all this, your motivation to help another should not emanate from the desire to receive, even though this remains an inevitability when you "Pass It On." Your motivation should derive from the fact that you genuinely like to see others succeeding. Even with The Boomerang Effect, the Law of the Farm, the Law of Cause and Effect, the Law of Karma, you have to realise that a certain amount of tough, unusual, challenging experiences will come your way automatically, simply by living on this planet. Why add to those painful experiences by sabotaging others?

Doing exactly what you want in life represents a gift. If you do not want others to have this gift, why should you have it? Why should you have anything you desire in your life, if you do not want others to get what they desire? You want a good man, give others what they want, on purpose! When you have this attitude, things will start to happen for you in a big way. They may not happen immediately, but if you keep on sowing in the right soil and stay persistent, they *will* happen. Always take actions to help someone else get what they want, do not hinder their progress. If you do not take these altruistic actions and then look back at your life wondering why you haven't achieved what you wanted or got the good man you want, you have only yourself to blame. Have you been selfish instead of selfless? Hurtful instead of helpful? Manipulative instead of mature? Your call.

Competition in life often stems from a desire for meaning and significance, sometimes even over personal joy. However, we have to take great care with competition. Seeing someone else promoted at a quicker rate than yourself can lead to bitterness, but personal development necessitates that you continuously work on yourself in such a way that upon hearing someone else's promotion, you can still experience true heartfelt and genuine joy for them. "Why not me?" does not represent a joyous attitude. You should have gratitude that you have the privilege of seeing someone else rise. After such a meteoric ascendancy, if you do not get a kick out of "I know him," or "I know her," as Plato said, you need to examine your life! If the person who has risen lives by the Laws and has the genuine heart, they will always say, "Hay, I know *you*." Achievement and promotion is more fun this way.

What does career satisfaction have to do with your acquisition of a good man? Simple, the Universe does not respond to categories? As in, give me this in my personal life, but keep my career life as it is or vice versa. If the Universe does not respond to categories neither should you. Gandhi said: "Life is one indivisible whole, you cannot do right in one department whilst still doing wrong in another." You cannot begrudge someone's career life and expect to progress in your own career and personal life. Once again, being continuously grateful for what you have and helping others achieve what they want, sets in motion a series of vibrational events that will bring you what you want…by Law!

The Instruction fulfills Box:

INSTRUCTIONS #7

A) The Law of Karma: You pass on good will. Good will literally overrun you sometimes. Some people wonder why certain individuals always seem to have great things happen to them. It's simply that in their past they invested selflessly in others and positive investments always have a pay off and a payday.

B) The Law of Cause and Effect: Every action has an equal and opposite reaction, this is in line with the law of Karma.

C) The Law of Expectation: When you throw goodwill out, by the Law of Karma, you should expect it to come back.

D) The Law of Correspondence: When goodwill becomes your method of operation, it will shine through in everything you do.

E) The Law of Being: You are goodwill. When you can reach a point when there exists not a malicious bone in your body, but instead a spirit of giving and helping, you will have arrived. However, you never arrive, life presents situations where you constantly have to go back to basics and remember the point of your existence. As Gandhi said: "Be the change you want to see."

My actions are my only true belongings. I cannot escape the consequences of my actions. My actions are the ground upon which I stand. - Thich Nhat Hanh

INSTRUCTION EIGHT

Understand Choice And

Responsibility Concepts

We are made wise not by the recollection of our past, but by the responsibility for our future. -George Bernard Shaw

INSTRUCTION EIGHT
UNDERSTAND CHOICE AND RESPONSIBILITY CONCEPTS

For purposes of exiting poetic license, this instruction fulfills every Law less the Law of Accident. Matter of factly, the Law of Accident doesn't figure in any instruction. You didn't even pick up this book by accident! Instead of telling you why this final instruction fulfills the Laws and why no instruction entails the Law of Accident, I'm going to let you do the work. I will say this though, from picking up this book to following the instructions, you are experiencing what happens when you live your life *on purpose*. On purpose-living means that there exist no accidents, there exist no coincidences. Can I leave you with that choice to make? Will you take on the responsibility to investigate this last instruction? You choose. Ladies, the whole of life finds peace in two words: "choice" and "responsibility." We may just wittle it down to one word, since you will always have a choice whether to take responsibility or not. Your life represents a collection of days and every day you have to make decisions which involves making a choice. If life in its simplest form encompasses a collection of decisions over time and you are responsible for your decisions, in this way then, you and you alone are ultimately responsible for your life. No one holds a gun to your head and demands that you enter a certain relationship, that remains always your decision, your choice. You have the ability to choose any course of action you want on any day: wake up, don't wake up, work out, don't work out, call your girlfriend, don't call your girlfriend, follow the instructions, don't follow the instructions. Once you understand that everything in life involves a choice, you will then easily understand that you and nobody else determines your life. I heave when I hear people blame God for their lives, if it's a good life, they did it themselves, if it's a bad life, from the day they were born, God had it in for them. Not so quick Sherlock. You, not God, made your life. Your life has always rested in your hands. When desirable men walk into your life, who pushes them away, you or God? When loser men and tap-dancer entertainers click clack their way into your life, who keeps them around, you or

God? Please shake loose of this ridiculous notion that the rich, happy, fulfilled woman next door who has the really intelligent kids has just had a string of good luck her whole life. No. Something she does daily and continues to do daily has created the environment she wants. Something she has done daily has allowed the friendly, dispassionate Universe to respond favorably. She has understood the choice and responsibility concepts. The same woman who told Dick Clark in 1983 that she wanted to rule the world is the same woman who twenty-five years later said: "We have total and complete control, influence, we are all in charge of our destiny and we're kidding ourselves if we think we're not." Madonna has ruled the music world as one of the best performance artists of all time. She married and eight years later, she decided to divorce. Her life, her choice. The same woman who said she became so obsessed with The Color Purple that she gave books to people on the street is the same woman who said: "I don't think of myself as a poor deprived ghetto girl who made good, I think of myself as someone who from a young age knew that I was responsible for myself and I had to make good." Oprah *is* television and radio broadcasting defined, she started with cents, has amassed billions and has had a life partner, as opposed to a "traditional" husband all these years. Her life, her choice.

Marriage, though a wonderful institution, has had record numbers of women running for the mountains screaming, not "Free ee Nelson Mandela," but instead, "Free ee mee!" Gabriele Pauli, twice divorced, told reporters what she thought about marriage at the launch of her campaign for entry into a German political party: "The basic approach is wrong...many marriages last just because people believe they are safe." She continued, "My suggestion is that marriages expire after seven years." After that time, Pauli said, couples should either agree to extend their marriage or it should automatically dissolve. She has a point. However, I go on record as saying that the woman who follows the instructions stands a better chance of having a marriage and relationship that will last because her daily regimen focuses on personal development which, by Law, will usher in the good man "who will stay because he wants to and not because a piece of paper that says he has to." If a woman doesn't meet a "keeper" man (the one to write home about), it must mean that she did not complete the instructions and if she didn't complete the instructions, she has no one to blame but herself. You are responsible for your life, you always have a choice. Our decisions decide our circumstances. There do exist those wilderness experiences where thoughtful, methodical planning can still land us in the thick of things, these occur by design to keep us humble and to ensure that we will always give credit not to ourselves, but to the One who gives us life. "I'm going to give you free reign to choose what you want to do with your life, but I want to be totally engaged in the process so as you never forget who's The Boss." So, you can tell yourself on the one hand, "It's all about me." But certainly on the other hand, "It's all about You." The Judeo-Christian calls the You, God; The Jehovah Witness calls the You, Jehovah; some call You, the Light; the Native American calls You, The Great Spirit; some call You, the Higher Self...listen ladies, you can call the You, Roger Rabbit if you want, as long as you truthfully acknowledge The One, The Orchestrator of the Universe! You must live as your own managing director, but simultaneously be completely answerable to The Global CEO.

The sooner you understand that you have the ability to literally "fix" your life and then look back owning Dr Maya Angelou's words, "I take responsibility for the time I take up and the space I occupy... yes I do," the sooner you will move forward. If you somehow believe that you just exist, as this mass collection of molecules and nerve endings, wandering around in a world where people eat, work, live and then die; if you believe this, then neither I nor this book can help you. Your decisions have your name on them, your life has your name on it. *Your* life. If you make a decision to heed these words and follow the instructions to the tee, well, you will know what to expect with confidence? If you do not embrace these words, you should also know what to expect? It remains a little remiss of me to say that the woman who does not read this book will not have a man by her side.

Women have married, had serious relationships and divorced, long before Instructions arrived on the scene. But there exists a problem today. "Therefore, the times we live in mean that you have to take measures that your grandmothers and great grandmothers did not have to consider." Remember that line? I have traveled around the world and I didn't think it possible to meet so many brilliant, talented, intelligent and attractive women who stand adamantly sick and tired about their man situation or lack thereof. As I said in "The Great Lie," I had to do something. My deep concern resulted in this, the second and final part of the romantic relationships' journey. Never in my life, have I felt such a responsibility to a group of people. I have done my part, now you go and do yours!

In conclusion, I want you to go down the line of history and look at the lives of the successful. Somewhere in their journeys, you will read something about them deciding to take responsibility for their lives. In Part One, I informed you about "The Three Great Women," Oprah, Dr Maya Angelou and Dr Aunty Jackie McCullough. Sudanese model Alek Wek similarly illustrates the responsibility mantra. After she arrived in London on a refugee visa, she went to school in Hackney, London. At school, due to her dark skin, they called her Midnight Black. Despite that she said: "But it was the first time in my life that I felt safe. I felt I could look towards the future and decide what I wanted to do." Wek made a decision to do whatever she needed to do in order to progress and her life moved forward in big ways. She won a scholarship to study Art and Design at the London Institute and paid for her materials by scrubbing loos at the BBC. Whilst getting "busy" with her life, a Models 1 Scout spotted her in Crystal Palace Park. Today, she is known as Supermodel Alek Wek. From Midnight Black to "please can you sign my shirt?" Well well. I need you to understand that when you decide to get up and move, refusing to sit "there" frustrated, sad, disgruntled, taking "life as it comes," resigned to spinsterhood, even though you do not want that resignation: when you take the responsibility and get active with a designed plan, you literally schedule your promotion or in this case, you schedule the good man into your life. Do you have the ability to want something so intensely, by controlling all that you possibly can, as the Captain of your own ship, polishing it, sharpening it and after you've done all to make it of its greatest value, walk to the engine room and just stand at the wheel. Do you have it in you to do all that work and then, as Oprah did with The Color Purple, surrender all to the friendly, dispassionate Universe, the Being of Meticulous and Exact Order. Do you have that ability? If you surely want a good man, you will find the ability!

I want to tell you that if you can just delight yourself in the Laws of the Universe, put your total trust and confidence in The Processes, acknowledging that they work, you will surely get your good man and he will be, just like from Part One, "as is best for you." Do not listen to the pundits, for they will probably say you cannot transform yourself in such quick time. Do not listen to your girlfriends, they may not have the courage to believe and expect as you do. Do not even listen to your feelings, because on that Monday morning just before a "busy" week at work, your feelings will have you sleep in, instead of going for that early morning run. No, just choose to take responsibility. When he arrives, determine in your mind that you will be ready and prepared to fulfill your part of the equation. They told Michelle Obama that her husband couldn't do it, that he was too young, too inexperienced and he had a funny name. "Who will vote for a guy named Barack Obama?" But you see, while those pundits were graduating from journalism and broadcasting school, sharpening not their saws but their critique hats, Michelle Obama remained "busy" getting on with her life. The pundits said no, but I can only imagine what "The Real Thing" thought. I can only imagine what this gravitassed, stable force in society told her good man: "I've been trained for this, your time is now. You need a rock to lean on, I am that rock. Yes You Can lean on me and Yes You Can do this." Will you have this mindset ladies when the good man walks into your life? It does not happen by osmosis, you have to bring this state into fruition. Michelle Obama, contrary to belief, does not hail from Mars, she is one of you. The good man, though confident in his abilities, having walked previous miles with supreme swagger, still knows that nothing Major League happens without the guidance and direction from a woman of excellence. "I've got a loud mouth, I tease my husband. He is incredibly smart and he is very able to deal with a strong woman, which is one of the reasons he can be President. He can deal with me." Ladies, this identifies one of the major reasons why you *will* have a good man by your side if you want to. *He* needs *you* and because *he* needs *you*, please just follow the cottin' pickin' instructions so he can find you. When you follow the instructions, it means I've done my job and I can invite Timothy back from sabbatical and the fun will really begin once again!

"With all that I am and all that I hope to be," as one Abraham Lincoln once said, "I owe to my angel mother." As I am the grateful son of one Hannah Johnson Oshinaike, the new-found nephew of one Aunty Jackie McCullough, the husband-theatrical pause-of one beautiful woman, the eager protégé of one Yanna Darili, Laurie Murray in Australia, Dr Mike Murdock, Paul Gambaccini and Mr Nels Armstrong, as Dartmouth Green is the color of perpetual hope and hope is dancing to the melody of a brighter future; as Dartmouth Green is the color of perpetual hope, I bid you DOOR SVEH DANYA, AY-FARISTON, and Thank you."

Thank you, thank you. You've been great. I think we have time for some questions. Yes, you in the green.

"Thank you so much Hanks. Will you be having this event yearly?"

"Well, I hope not (laughs from the crowd). I've put everything down here for you all so that I will not have to hold these too many times. Between this and "The Great Lie," I think you'll be set. I do like presenting before a live audience though. So I leave it open.

"Do you have any other projects coming up?"

"Well TV yes! There is a TV project which is ongoing, looking to get that commissioned soon. My next major written project involves a woman who has done more than she even knows. It's probably my biggest and most challenging project to date because I want to tell her story, just as though she was telling it herself. She has some major influences, her influences alone are books in themselves. I want to give great life to her influences in the book. I am studying now to show myself approved and worthy to do it. The enormity of her contribution to the world does add some pressure...and I know I will need more than just peanuts and chicken to keep me calm (laughs from the audience).

"Timothy" (shout from the crowd).

"Yes Timothy!! That's right. Last week he wrote me. Let me see if I can just find it...now where did I put it? Oh here it is. 'Hay Hanks, how you doing my alter-ego? Well I hope. I'm having a great time. I've traveled a tiny bit, just trying to brush up on my Foreign Affairs. For these last few months though I've stayed at home because I can see Russia from my house. Catch you later.'"

ENDNOTES

1. Faludi, Susan. *Backlash*. New York. Doubleday. 1991
2. ibid.
3. ibid.
4. Hill, Napoleon. Think and Grow Rich. London. Vermillion. 2004
5. Front Row with Hanks, The Great Lie. South Carolina. Booksurge. 2007.
6. ibid.
7. ibid.
8. CBS 60 Minutes 11/16/08
9. Reagan, Nancy. My Turn. New York. Random House. 1989.
10. Reagan, Nancy. I Love You, Ronnie. New York. Random House. 2002.
11. ibid.
12. Reagan, Nancy. My Turn. New York. Random House
13. Reagan, Nancy. I Love You, Ronnie
14. ibid.
15. Reagan, Nancy. My Turn. New York. Random House
16. ibid.
17. Belenky Field, M., Clincy McVicker., B., Goldberger Rule N., & Tarule Mattuck J. *Women's Ways of Knowing*. New York. Basic Books. 1986.

AUTHOR'S NOTE:

We at Front Row are dedicated to helping you, the individual and company attain exactly what you want in life, business or family. Whether you're the high-powered executive, green-eyed college student, aspiring athlete or "irritated" woman awaiting your Knight's arrival, these entertaining, interactive and multimedia presentations provide answers. Come sit Front Row, to not only tap your feet, but also embark on a long and winding journey. "You will have to disembark at the designated pit stops for fresh air, an oxygen mask and no doubt some Evian, but after that, The Home Straight will be in sight. I look forward to the privilege of seeing you...Front Row." Please log on to the website www.frontrowwithhanks.com for the 5 Front Rows and Center Court with Hanks-Basketball, testimonials, and description of programs. All Front Row presentations include extensive Q&A as time allows.

For Booking Information in the USA for seminars and speaking engagements: please fill out the mail form on the Contact page of the Front Row website or email contact@frontrowwithhanks.com

If you would like to schedule Center Court with Hanks-All Sports/Basketball for presentations and team consultancy, or specific basketball presentations and personal basketball training, both in and out of season, please fill out the mail form on the Center Court of the Front Row website or email centercourt@frontrowwithhanks.com

To send Hanks a message directly fill out the mail form on the Contact page of the Front Row website.

"I hope that your life will never be the same."

"I ACKNOWLEDGE"

I want to acknowledge Dean Cowart for his incredible design capabilities. Dean, you are one of the best! I named Dean first because it means I can say what follows without having to cover myself. Women, for all of their excellence, have the ability to take a vision and make it happen. In this project (and previously) The Great Lie, I am deeply grateful to Sarah Lange Davis who actually said that I didn't have to mention her. Sorry Sarah, you are too competent to leave out! In the same way, Laura Bonam, Danielle Cain-Stone, Jacqueline Volz, Nicole Briggs and Tara Schuley made this project both smooth and enjoyable. Can you not tell by their names that things get done when they hang up their coats in the morning and get down to work? Thank you ladies, thank you!